I0558271

Conspiracy Theories

The Secret Dark Side of History's Most Famous Events

(Final Warning the Digital Citizen the New World Order Box Set)

Arvel Herman

Published By **Elena Holly**

Arvel Herman

All Rights Reserved

Conspiracy Theories: The Secret Dark Side of History's Most Famous Events (Final Warning the Digital Citizen the New World Order Box Set)

ISBN   978-1-998927-96-8

No part of this guidebook shall be reproduced in any form without permission in writing from the publisher except in the case of brief quotations embodied in critical articles or reviews.

Legal & Disclaimer

The information contained in this book is not designed to replace or take the place of any form of medicine or professional medical advice. The information in this book has been provided for educational & entertainment purposes only.

The information contained in this book has been compiled from sources deemed reliable, and it is accurate to the best of the Author's knowledge; however, the Author cannot guarantee its accuracy and validity and cannot be held liable for any errors or omissions. Changes are periodically made to this book. You must consult your doctor or get professional medical advice before using any of the suggested remedies, techniques, or information in this book.

Table Of Contents

Chapter 1: Princess Diana

On the night time of August 31, 1997, Princess Diana died after a excessive-pace automobile crash within the Pont d'Alma tunnel in Paris. Diana changed into visiting within the lower decrease lower back of a car with Dodi Al-Fayed (son of billionaire Mohamed Al-Fayed). In the the the the front seats were bodyguard Trevor-Rees Jones and the Hotel Ritz's performing protection supervisor, Henri Paul. Henri Paul who became searching for to elude the paparazzi cars and motorcycles that were in pursuit of the auto. Crashed right into a resource column in the tunnel, and subsequently all but Jones died from their accidents.

Her lack of life on the age of 36 induced a global show of grief.

French government investigated the case and judged it an accident, because of Henri Paul's reckless riding at the same time as underneath the have an impact on of antidepressants and alcohol (3 times the criminal restrict in France).

However, Mohamed Al-Fayed has insinuated that Prince Philip, The Prince of Wales, Diana's sister Lady Sarah McCorquodale and numerous others have been all worried in a plot to kill the Princess and his son.

Henri Paul

An evaluation of blood samples, have been stated to consist of an alcohol diploma that become 3 times the French crook limit.

Henri Paul's blood changed into switched on the morgue?

There have been claims that the blood used to test his alcohol degree at the time of the crash end up in reality now not his, however changed into switched with a suicide victim who modified into within the morgue that night time time, who had died of carbon monoxide poisoning. After all there had been immoderate degrees of carbon monoxide in his blood.

Well one test showed a excessive degree and a few one-of-a-kind one a confirmed low stage - so averaged out pretty regular. He also smoked cigars that night time time time which could probably have multiplied the carbon monoxide in his blood.

DNA samples, authenticated with the aid of the use of a evaluation with samples furnished with the aid of Paul's dad and mom, showed the blood samples which contained excessive alcohol ranges have been from Henri Paul.

French authorities moreover finished each different test on the fluid from the sclera (white of the attention). This showed now not only the identical prevent cease end result however additionally that Paul had been taking antidepressants.

CCTV photographs of Paul simply earlier than leaving the Ritz that nighttime proved that he regarded regular to most (despite the truth that now not all) of folks that noticed him that night.

Professor Robert Forrest, a forensic pathologist, stated that many humans, in particular people with a higher tolerance for alcohol, appear greater sober than they honestly are. Not all alcoholics in form into the stereotypical inebriated of slurring and swaying about.

How need to he have presently emerge as a certified pilot, which incorporates exams for alcohol abuse?

Europe-vast standards for pilots' medicals in 1997 required no particular clinical test for alcoholism. Often a smooth self-certification of alcohol problems changed into all that modified into required from pilots.

Henri Paul's non-public vehicle turn out to be an automated antique fashion mini and that night time time he became driving a guide Mercedes with 193 hp and 0 - 100km/h in 10 seconds. Moreover he became the use of below a cocktail of drink and anti-depressants, at sixty one-sixty three miles in step with hour, two times the fee restrict right into a tunnel that were the scene of 34 crashes and 8 deaths within the previous 15 years. Senior accident investigator Anthony Read said he want to "almost guarantee" that the couple should have survived had they been strapped in and traveling at the rate restriction whilst their Mercedes crashed in Paris's Alma tunnel.

Conspiracy theorists declare that Paul changed right into a thriller provider agent and that he became paid to homicide Princess Diana and Dodi Al Fayed at the orders of the British Establishment.

Ok they very last cracked it - he have end up a suicidal carrier agent!

The Fiat Uno

What approximately the Fiat Uno which brought approximately the Mercedes to swerve and thereby crash into the element of the tunnel and grow to be never traced?

Al-Fayed alleged that the Fiat Uno became owned via way of a French photojournalist named Jean-Paul James Andanson. A protection offerings agent regular with Fayed,

Andanson had been interviewed by means of the usage of French police in February 1998, and become capable of offer airline tickets and toll road receipts as evidence of his whereabouts. It became moreover established that his Fiat Uno grow to be off the road at the time, resting on bricks at his home a hundred seventy miles a long way from Paris.

To endorse that MI6 may plan to murder Diana the use of a Fiat Uno to gently faucet a heavy Mercedes S-Class off the street is pretty some distance fetched. Moreover, it's incredulous that Anderson ought to have used a car registered in his private call to intentionally purpose this fatal coincidence.

It's likely that the Fiat Uno belonged to Le Van Thanh, a Vietnamese plumber and night time time watchman. His failure to prevent at the scene of an twist of future, non-public up and the speedy repainting of his vehicle, may be defined as an immigrant afraid of having entangled in French regulation.

There have been no CCTV pics from the Ritz resort right as plenty because the deadly collision.

The 10 video cameras at the direction taken through manner of using the Mercedes were everyday private protection cameras coping with the entrances to homes, now not the sort that factor on the site visitors, for this reason that that they had no applicable photos. The CCTV in the tunnel come to be grew to grow to be off. This can also additionally moreover sound absurd, and possibly it's miles, but it became popular workout after 11pm. It wasn't specially have come to be off that night time.

Oh and you could have heard about a 'CCTV' photo that end up published in a e-book through David Cohen, 'Diana, Death of a Goddess' as having been taken just earlier than the auto entered the tunnel. How ought to this be while the CCTVs had been seemingly all have become off? This picture is referred to now to have been eager about the resource of using the paparazzi at the same time as the Mercedes changed into using away from the Ritz Hotel. Not a CCTV nevertheless.

Some confused why changed into the tunnel wiped clean and opened up another time after simplest 4 hours?

Well all the proof had been gathered, there was no reason to maintain it closed any similarly as some shape of shrine.

The adventure to the health center

Why did it take nearly hours from the time the emergency services arrived until arriving at the health center?

Ok this dreams breaking down a piece to get a clearer photo of the timeline:

12:26 am -name to the emergency offerings' switchboard.

12:30 am Police Officers arrive

12:forty am Doctor Jean-Marc Martino, a expert in anaesthetics and extensive care remedy and the medical medical doctor in price of the SAMU ambulance arrive.

1:00am Diana turn out to be eliminated from the auto and suffered cardiac arrest.

1:18 am She emerge as moved to the SAMU ambulance

1:41 am The ambulance departed the crash scene

2:06 am She arrived on the Pitié-Salpêtrière hospital (this 25 minute adventure protected a prevent on the way because of the drop within the blood strain).

The ambulance became visiting slowly because the medical doctor was involved approximately the Diana's blood pressure and the consequences on her clinical circumstance of deceleration and acceleration of the automobile.

Yes however there have been 2 important hospitals closer the crash web web site. Why no longer cross instantly to at least one of those?

Thierry Merrese medical institution authorities said that Parisian hospitals rotate on an emergency responsibility roster. That night time time the Pitié-Salpêtrière Hospital become the primary reception centre for multiple trauma patients in Paris. They had the remarkable surgeons on standby, which encompass Professor Bruno Riou who changed into on obligation on the Pitié-Salpêtrière that night time time and became in particular expert to deal with her accidents.

Her relationship with Dodi

Diana and Dodi Fayed had been approximately to announce their engagement?

The marriage of the mother of the future king and a high-quality Egyptian Muslim might also surely now not be tolerated and she or he had to be murdered.

Not regular with humans she knew. On Friday 29 August, truly days in advance than the twist of destiny, Diana's eldest sister, Lady Sarah McCorquodale said that Diana gave her the impact the connection come to be in reality on "stony floor".

Friends who had these days spoken to Diana, which incorporates her butler Paul Burrell, her buddy Lady Annabel Goldsmith and her spiritual adviser Rita Rogers all stated that she had absolutely no purpose of turning into engaged or married to every body at that factor.

There changed into also no evidence decided of any education having been made to announce an engagement. Big bulletins which include this requires big steerage in arranging a press conference.

Besides, Diana had formerly had a 12 months courting with Hasnat Khan, a Muslim coronary coronary coronary heart doctor of Pakistani starting region. Diana had explored the possibility of marriage with him. Hasnat Khan stated that this had been met and now not using a competition from the Royal Family and Prince Charles had truly given his blessing.

Mohamed Al Fayed said that Dodi had already provided the engagement ring from the Alberto Repossi jewellers.

When CCTV evidence inside the jewellers modified into checked out it showed that Dodi left Alberto Repossi jewellers on the 30 August with best a list.

The maintain assistant, Claude Roulet, additionally contradicted the assertion.

Pregnancy

Diana became pregnant.

In May 2001 Mohamed Al Fayed claimed that Diana advised him, in a cellphone name on August 31 1997, that she changed into pregnant with Dodi's child.

First of all it is not possible that Mohamed Al Fayed might have stored this a thriller for three and a half of years in advance than telling the press.

Secondly Diana's buddies who knew her menstrual cycle also said that she could not had been pregnant on the time of her loss of life.

Thirdly, Coroner Dr. John Burton, stated that he attended a post-mortem exam of the Princess's body at Fulham mortuary, wherein he in my view tested her womb and decided her now not to be pregnant.

Surely Diana's frame became deliberately embalmed with illegal haste after her death, making it not feasible to perform a being pregnant test to reveal whether or now not or now not or now not she have come to be carrying Dodi's toddler.

The embalming modified into ordered with the aid of manner of the close by police. Her body become starting to grow to be worse within the past due summer time warmness and it therefore would have been unacceptable to provide her to Charles, Diana's sisters and the French President Jacques Chirac who may speedy be viewing the frame.

Furthermore, in accordance the French doctors, the princess, at the request of her family, changed into great in component embalmed. Partial embalming is a not unusual manner to preserve the body for classy functions and professionals argue it'd not corrupt being pregnant assessments.

Robert Thompson, manager Fulham mortuary, said that a partial embalming did not have an effect at the legs or decrease 1/2 of of the frame together with the uterus and concluded on inspection that she have turn out to be no longer pregnant.

Scientific exams had been also finished on pre-transfusion blood positioned inside the destroyed automobile and determined to haven't any hint of the HCG hormone associated with being pregnant.

Al Fayed asserted that Diana and his son had spent hours with an indoors style clothier, journeying a villa he owned in Paris to pick out a room "for the little one".

A safety protect on the villa, Reuben Murrell, later stated that the visit lasted a whole lot a whole lot much less than thirty minutes. He furnished stills from CCTV to reveal this. Whilst within the presence of Diana and Dodi for everything in their visit, he had no recollection of a conversation about them coming to live on the villa.

Further feedback.

Any planned conspiracy may additionally need to had to have acknowledged that;

Dodi can also need to make the very last-minute alternate of plan that night time.

Henri Paul could be the driving stress

Henri Paul might be beneath the have an effect on of alcohol and drugged

He might take that specific course to Dodi's condo

Dodi and Diana might not placed on seat belts

Imagine how many people may had to have colluded in bloodless blooded murder - which consist of medical doctors, nurses and ambulance drivers not to say the unreliability of assassination thru vehicle crash.

Chapter 2: The Apollo Eleven Moon Landings

In the late Nineteen Fifties,the space race can also grow to be a opposition a number of america and the Soviet Union attempt to show the superiority of its era. President John F. Kennedy made the claim that the U.S. Would land someone at the moon earlier than the end of the decade. On July 16, 1969, after a few years of experiments, check flights, and education the Apollo 11 spacecraft have become released from Cape Kennedy into space. Apollo 11 emerge as the primary manned assignment to land at the Moon. The group, astronauts Neil Armstrong, Buzz Aldrin, and Michael Collins. Set off at the number one lunar landing attempt. On July 20, 1969 Neil Armstrong and Buzz Aldrin moved to the Lunar module, referred to as the Eagle, and started out their descent to the Moon. Armstrong needed to land the module manually, after which he stepped outdoor and have become the number one guy to walk at the

Moon. He famously referred to as the immediately "...One small step for someone, one massive leap for mankind". The astronauts efficiently again to Earth with forty seven.Five kilos of samples from some different planetary frame.

The Photographs

No stars are visible in the images taken thru manner of the Apollo astronauts from the floor of the Moon.

The Apollo landing takes area all through lunar mornings, with the Sun shining brightly. Furthermore, the cameras had been set for daylight publicity, so the stars had been not vibrant enough on this light to be captured within the pics.

David Groves, PhD, has confirmed that the x-ray surroundings of vicinity could short render any photographs unusable.

Dr. Groves did no longer use in his checks the equal Hasselblad EL/500 or EL/seven hundred camera Apollo undertaking camera.

The Hasselblad had additional thicker safety to the movie magazines for the duration of the mission. Dr. Groves does no longer record any similar safety to his film magazine.

He provided absolutely no protective across the film throughout its publicity to the x-rays and he exposed the movie to x-rays loads of instances extra immoderate than what takes place in vicinity. It is likewise doubtful whether or not he left the film indoors its magazine due to the truth the Apollo astronauts might have completed.

It gets up to 280 F (138 C) at the moon and film melts at 150 F (sixty five C).

Firstly, air temperature has no because of this at the moon due to the truth there may be no air.

Furthermore Dr. Groves makes use of an oven to warmth the film. An oven uses by and massive convective warm temperature transfer: the element heats the air within the oven and the air then transfers the warmth to the fabric being cooked. As there can be no air at the moon, no such convective warmth transfer occurs.

How might also need to the astronauts manipulate the sensitive controls of the cameras in those clumsy gloves?

The Hasselblad cameras were modified to be operated while carrying area gloves and to go through the lunar environment. For instance, the shutter release button grow to be enlarged notably. So large in truth that the astronauts took inadvertent pictures because of by means of twist of destiny pressing the shutter release button.

One NASA image is calling up at Neil Armstrong approximately to take his huge step for mankind from the moon floor. Who took the photo?

There grow to be an arm connected to the lander which had a tv and a although digital camera installation to it.

The heavy landing module sits on top of the sand making no impact. Yet there are snap shots of the astronaut's footprints inside the identical sand.

The touchdown module sits on the robust rock. The dust, having been blown apart thru the blast, after which it settled once more. The astronauts then started out their moonwalk wherein the dust had settled.

How can also want to the footprints in the brilliant lunar dirt be so well preserved, at the same time as there may be no moisture or environment. Almost as even though made in wet sand?

Anything finely powdered will clump together while packed tightly. Plus the lack of wind meant that the dry lunar dirt isn't blown away.

Von Braun

Conspiracists argue that Marshall Space Flight Center Director Wernher von Braun's experience to Antarctica in 1967 modified into to build up lunar meteorites to be used as faux Moon rocks.

The truth that there might be pretty some meteorites in Antarctica grow to be first considered in 1969 through Japanese scientists. This have become years after von Braun went there.

Antarctic lunar meteorite wasn't observed until 1979 and wasn't even known for it's lunar beginning place until 1982.

380 kilograms of Moon rocks had been amassed with the aid of NASA among 1969 and 1972 but handiest approximately 30 kilograms of lunar meteorites were positioned on Earth up until the late 1990s -

19 specimens, regardless of non-public lenders and governmental corporations worldwide seeking out greater than two decades. It makes it difficult for NASA to have gathered 380 kilograms for the Apollo 11 and 12 missions and put together them on this kind of brief time frame.

Take Off

When the landing module takes to the air from the Moon's floor there's no visible flame from the rocket.

The rockets inside the touchdown module are powered with the aid of way of gasoline containing a aggregate of hydrazine and dinitrogen tetroxide, they ignite with out the want for a spark and burn and no longer the usage of a visible flame.

On Earth, the more gasoline burns in touch with atmospheric oxygen, enhancing the visible flame. This cannot show up in a vacuum.

The Flag

When the astronauts are putting in place the American flag, it waves. Yet there can be no wind on the Moon.

The flagpole is made of mild, flexible aluminium and motion photographs show that after the astronauts permit move of the flagpole it vibrates in brief, giving the affect of blowing in the wind, then remains still. There is not every different indication of wind together with dirt blowing spherical.

What about the apparent waving movement inside the nevertheless pics?

The flag itself have become made from a totally slight nylon and retained the rippled have an effect on from being scrunched tightly in its packaging. Especially so in the lunar gravity.

Why is the American flag constantly seem like lit up?

Nylon flags usually will be predisposed to glow while backlit.

The Van Allen Belt

The astronauts couldn't have survived the adventure due to exposure to radiation from the Van Allen radiation belt.

The quick time it takes to skip through the belt, combined with the protection from the spacecraft, technique any exposure to radiation can be very low.

Dr James Van Allen himself said "The declare that radiation publicity within the route of the Apollo missions could have been lethal to the astronauts is excellent one instance of such nonsense."

The danger of the Van Allen belts is high-power protons, which aren't that tough to guard towards. The Apollo navigators plotted the trajectory to pass fast through the thinnest elements (the rims) of the belts, limiting the exposure.

Six feet of lead is wanted to protect toward the Van Allen belt radiation.

Six toes of lead might likely shield in the direction of a totally massive atomic explosion or defend against excessive, excessive-frequency electromagnetic radiation. That isn't the equal form of the radiation placed in the Van Allen belt. In the Van Allen belt, using heavy dense metallic protecting is genuinely counterproductive in protective in opposition to particle radiation. Polyethylene is greater powerful. The fibrous insulation between the inner and outer hulls of the command module changed into likely the exceptional form of radiation protecting in competition to particles, as this isn't always much like shielding towards rays.

The Apollo's steering pc strength changed into equivalent of truely one in every of extremely-modern-day kitchen home equipment.

Just due to the truth computing electricity has now advanced while you do not forget that then, doesn't recommend that it changed into inadequate for going to the moon in 1969.

Further feedback.

The Soviet Academy of Sciences geologists tested Apollo lunar samples and characteristic acknowledged that the Apollo programme have become a easy success.

The Soviet spacecraft format, which changed into to have carried cosmonauts to the moon, did now not provide a meter of lead for his or her spacecraft every.

How may also additionally need to a whole department of technology has been fooled or suppressed global for many years via the U.S. Government that allows you to guard its mystery?

At the peak of the Apollo venture nearly half of a million people had been strolling on it.

Yet in over thirty years, not one individual has come ahead to say he modified into part of the conspiracy and provide incontestable evidence for it.

Since the late 2000s, immoderate-definition pictures taken through the Lunar Reconnaissance Orbiter (LRO) of the Apollo landing net web sites have captured the lander modules and the tracks left thru the use of the astronauts. Images have also been launched showing 5 of the six Apollo missions' American flags on the Moon. The satisfactory exception is that of Apollo 11, which changed into with the aid of twist of fate blown over via the takeoff rocket's exhaust.

Chapter 3: Martin Luther King

On Thursday, April four, 1968, King become staying at the Lorraine Motel in Memphis. A Radio and TV bulletin added that King turn out to be staying in room quantity 306. James Earl Ray, rented a room during from the Lorraine Motel which ignored the room in which King end up staying. Ray had rejected the number one room he modified into furnished-it didn't have a view of the Lorraine.

Shortly in advance than 6pm., King had long past out onto the balcony and at one minute beyond six, Ray, the usage of a rifle with a sniper scope, fired the unmarried shot that ended King's lifestyles.The unmarried bullet fired from a Remington Model 760, severed King's spinal cord and killed him. King became rushed to St. Joseph's Hospital wherein he modified into stated useless at 7:05pm. That nighttime.

Moments later witnesses said seeing someone, later believed to be James Earl

Ray, fleeing from a rooming residence during the street from the Lorraine Motel. Ray panicked at the equal time as he observed police motors parked in a close-by hearth station. He then threw a package deal containing the rifle, in competition to a shop front. Police discovered the package deal and inner Ray's fingerprints were positioned on multiple binoculars and the rifle, which facts showed he had offered six days earlier than the taking pix.

The FBI later, located Ray's fingerprints on diverse devices left in the rest room from wherein the gunfire had come from. A manhunt ensued and months after King's loss of lifestyles, he come to be arrested at Heathrow Airport trying to depart the United Kingdom, after he had robbed a London financial organization. Ray changed into fast extradited to Tennessee and charged with King's murder.

To keep away from an ordeal conviction and the possibility of a loss of life penalty, he confessed to the assassination on March 10, 1969. As a end give up result, an ordeal became waived and Ray became given a 99-yr jail sentence. Despite having suggested the select out he understood that a accountable plea could not be appealed, he recanted his confession 3 days later.

On the advice of his lawyer, Percy Foreman, Ray took a accountable plea and changed into sentenced to 99 years in the Tennessee State Penitentiary. Ray later made many tries to withdraw his accountable plea and be tried with the useful aid of a jury. Despite many appeals, none of Ray's severa attorneys ever produced evidence convincing a court docket docket of law to reopen the case. Until he died in prison on April 23, 1998, on the age of 70, Ray maintained his innocence.

US Government set -up

William Pepper, Ray's closing legal professional, claims that Ray changed into installation via the U.S. Government.

They seemingly hired a Mafia hit guy to kill King and had Green Beret snipers close by as lower back up, need to the Mafia hit man miss. The squad have become known as Alpha 184. The CIA, the Memphis police, the FBI, and Army intelligence were also involved. Pepper claimed the commando of the Green Beret snipers, Billy Eidson, grow to be then killed off to maintain the plot mystery.

There was no Alpha 184 unit in lifestyles in 1968.

Green Beret Billy Eidson changed into located to be alive and nicely.

A replica of army orders Pepper used to prove the life of the special unit and the operation in opposition to King became a forgery.

The King own family were satisfied their grow to be a central authority plot.

On an version of ABC's Turning Point on June 19th 1997, Coretta Scott King and severa of the King kids added their belief in Ray's innocence and the lifestyles of a government plot. Dexter King maintained that Army intelligence, the CIA, the FBI and Lyndon Johnson had been answerable for his father's loss of life.

A Hit Man

According to LloydJowers, Ray became best a scapegoat and no longer straight away concerned within the taking photographs.

in 1968 Lloyd Jowers, ran Jim's Grill which became positioned all through the street from the Lorraine Motel. In 1993, Lloyd Jowers appeared on ABC's Prime Time Live claiming an alleged conspiracy related to the Mafia, the U.S. Authorities and himself to kill King. He also claimed that Frank Liberto, a Memphis produce provider (now vain), gave him $a hundred,000 to hire a success guy to murder King—and the killer he employed wasn't Ray.

Jowers saved converting the story. Since 1993 he claimed that the shooter become:

African American man.

Raul.

A white "Lieutenant" with the Memphis Police Department.

A character whom he did not understand.

In 1999, the King own family filed a civil case inside the path of Jowers and unnamed co-conspirators and received.

The case became attempted inside the circuit courtroom docket of Shelby County, Tennessee, from November 15 to December 8, 1999. Attorney William Francis Pepper, representing the King own family, furnished 'proof' alleging government involvement. The jury concluded that King were the victim of assassination thru way of a conspiracy concerning Loyd Jowers, the Memphis police as well as federal companies. The accepted quantity of damages furnished to the the King circle of relatives (the plaintiffs) have become 100 dollars.

No authorities officers or agencies have been named or made a celebration to the in form, so there has been no defence or evidence presented or refuted with the aid of way of way of the government. Only testimony and pleadings submitted through the plaintiffs and Jowers.

Local assistant district legal professional John Campbell said that the case "not noted lots contradictory evidence that in no way changed into supplied".

In 2000, the Department of Justice finished their very very own research into Jowers' claims; it did now not find proof to help the allegations.

The sisters whom Pepper claimed had worked in Jowers's restaurant and had corroborated his story, later admitted the story have become fake.

Jowers had 3 specific witnesses

Betty Spates

James McCraw

John McFerren

Betty Spates testified that she became on the eating place at the same time as King emerge as shot and she or he or he noticed Jowers protective a rifle and that he ultimately knowledgeable her it changed into the rifle he used to kill King.

Betty Spates come to be not amongst the ones found in Jowers's diner from whom the police took statements.

She later changed her mind approximately the whole tale that Jowers had killed King. She informed her sister that she nice informed the story because Jowers had promised her a reduce of the earnings from his e-book and movie rights about the affair.

James McCraw a cab motive force who claimed to had been despatched to the rooming residence to select out up a fare and noticed the second one floor rest room in which Ray shot MLK end up empty.

Records from the taxi agency in 1968 display that McCraw had no fare at the boarding house on the day of the assassination.

John McFerren claimed that he overheard Frank Liberto, apparently with Mafia ties, take a smartphone call from James Earl Ray and ordered him to "shoot the bastard at the balcony" an hour earlier than the assassination.

McFerren's statements have changed through the years and do no longer in form what he stated in 1968.

Raul

What approximately this guy named Raul. I concept there has been evidence that he did it?

Ray fired his attorney and stated via his new felony professional Jack Kershaw that notwithstanding the fact that he did now not "in my opinion shoot King", he can also additionally have been "in element accountable with out expertise it". He now claimed to had been framed with the resource of the usage of a latin guy he met in Montreal named "Raul" or "Raoul", with whom he have end up worried in smuggling operations. This Raul suggested him to buy the rifle, which was located at the murder scene and test into the rooming residence opposite the Lorraine Motel. Ray didn't ask why. The night time time in advance than the assassination, Ray exceeded the rifle over to Raul and has not met him due to the fact. Raoul, or a person with Raoul's assistance, then shot King from there, leaving the rifle with Ray's prints at the scene.

His story stored changing.

In a few specific version, he changed into ready in a car outside the boardinghouse from which the fatal shot modified into fired even as Raoul ran out, jumped into the automobile and guarded himself with a white sheet.

In some other Ray said Raoul became with him on the equal time as he furnished the rifle.

Ray wasn't even there whilst King became murdered.

Attorney Jack Kershaw claimed Ray modified into some region else whilst the pictures have been fired.

He couldn't find out a single witness to corroborate this claim.

Ray said Raoul stayed at a resort in Mississippi.

Every lodge in the region have become checked and no hint of every body matching Raoul's description end up observed.

Didn't they locate Raul living in New York?

Ray's prison expert confident that new investigators had in the end located Raul. A female named Glenda Grabow stated that he had bragged to her that he had killed King.

The guy end up traced and he transpired to be a retired autoworker. He labored for the identical car employer company for almost 30 years.He have been with the equal agency for 30 years and became at art work at the day of the killing. Until 1980 he had in no way long gone everywhere else inside the United States besides for one enjoy to Portland, Ore. He has never even been to Texas or Tennessee and he had in no manner met Glenda Grabow.

Grabow stated that no longer nice grow to be Raoul have become a friend of Jack Ruby, however he had also killed President Kennedy.

Jack Ruby changed into by no means in Houston, the city in which Grabow claimed she knew Raoul.

Further observation.

When he have become 17, Ray joined the Army, became infatuated with Adolf Hitler and asked to be stationed in Germany.

In jail he changed into supplied a flow into to an honor farm however became it down because of the reality the dormitories were racially included.

In 1960, Ray, who emerge as then within the Missouri State Penitentiary, began boasting that there was cash to be made in killing black leaders like H. Rap Brown, Stokely Carmichael, and King.

Ray shocked his brothers saying "I'm going to kill that n——King..."..."That's some issue it is been on my mind. That's a few issue I've been running on."

At the time of the assassination, Ray changed proper right into a fugitive; he had escaped almost a year earlier on the equal time as serving a 20-yr sentence for armed theft (his fourth conviction).

A federal research in 1977–1978 by the House Select Committee on Assassinations concluded that even though "there's a chance" that Ray did no longer act alone in planning the assassination, he on my own pulled the cause.

Ray had purchased the rifle beneath an alias six days earlier.

That Ray has lived 30 years after the homicide is persuasive proof that specialists had been now not involved. If they had been, they'll have disposed of Ray prolonged ago--so long as he became alive, he may also want to have have become on them. Ray's felony professional, Jack Kershaw, additionally happy Ray to take a polygraph test as a part of an interview with Playboy. The magazine said that the check effects showed "that Ray did, in fact, kill Martin Luther King . And that he did so by myself.

He bought the Remington 760 Gamemaster rifle that killed MLK and had it geared up with the 2x7 scope.

Ray's fingerprints were recovered from the identical rifle he had himself offered.

A map, decided inside the room he rented, had circles drawn close to King's former domestic, the Southern Christian Leadership Conference headquarters, Ebenezer Baptist Church and the Capitol Homes Housing Project, where Ray abandoned his Mustang after the assassination.

The proof toward him is overwhelming. He hated black human beings. ''We want to kill them, kill all of them," a chum quoted him as saying. He grow to be a career criminal, an armed robber, He was an high-quality shot with a rifle.

Ray stalked King for days earlier than the homicide. He went to Memphis whilst the newspapers said that King have come to be going there.

James Earl Ray failed separate lie detector tests even as questioned on if he shot MLK. (When at a loss for words if he changed into part of a conspiracy, Ray replied no in each tests; one examiner concluded Ray have grow to be lying, within the 2nd check the examiner concluded the results had been ambiguous).

In the commonplace version of the assassination—one that no credible historian, or federal or nation research has ever disputed, a career crook and open racist, murdered Martin Luther King on April 4, 1968.

Chapter 4: 11th Of September

On the morning of 11th of September 2001, 19 militants related to the Islamic extremist organization al-Qaeda hijacked 4 airplanes and carried out suicide attacks towards goals within the United States. Without giving away their intentions the flight controls had been taken over and two of the planes had been flown into the twin towers of the World Trade Center in New York City, a third aircraft hit the Pentagon sincerely outdoor Washington, D.C., and the fourth aircraft, perception with the aid of way of a few to were intended for the White House modified into crashed, thru passenger interference, in a topic in Pennsylvania.

The attacks resulted inside the complete crumble of the World Trade Center dual towers in New York City and heavy harm to at the least one factor of the Pentagon. Almost three,000 human beings were killed.

Delayed Response

The government deliberately held off to allow the carnage spread.

Prior to September 11 certainly all hijacking incidents concerning business plane had been for the motive of hostage-taking. This supposed FAA (The Federal Aviation Administration) believed that a skyjacked plane may also want to necessarily land someplace and negotiations for the hostages should start. Using anti-aircraft guns to shoot down passenger planes entire of humans grow to be not some issue that the authorities had even considered.

NORAD (The North American Aerospace Defence Command) didn't definitely music flights indoors America previous to 9/11. Advanced caution systems saved a lookout for incoming threats from outdoor the U.S. Wherein there's masses of time to scramble opponents to prevent bombers.

It fell on the Federal Aviation Administration (FAA) and the FBI to maintain their eyes on

American skies. Those businesses do not have planes they're capable of scramble.

The hijackers have grow to be off the transponders on their planes, which intended they couldn't be tracked. And NORAD desired an alert from Air Traffic Control to behave. So essentially, you had a device which ensured bureaucratic bungles, but that is a miles cry from complicit officials.

In slight of those activities warplanes are sincerely extra ready to shield in competition to this unique shape of attack. In addition, upgrades to monitoring abilties now allow the FAA and NORAD to extra simply realise while a few thing is incorrect and intercept quicker.

Flying Skills

They really didn't have the capabilities to efficiently guide those planes into three out of 4 goals.

They didn't ought to fly in horrible weather, take off, or land.

All were knowledgeable in car-pilot and navigational structures,

All four had expert and earned personal pilot's licenses.

One additionally had each a personal and commercial license, and experience with small business plane.

Controlled Demolition

The WTC houses had been deliberately destroyed through a controlled demolition. They fell right away down into their private footprint.

Controlled demolitions usually begin with the decrease tales being removed first. Photographic evidence shows World Trade Centre homes failed immoderate up wherein the planes struck and the decrease floors have been nonetheless intact till they were destroyed from above. In a managed explosion, demolition professionals disintegrate a constructing from the lowest no longer the pinnacle.

Once each tower started out to crumble, the burden of all of the floors commenced out collapse downward thru the constructing in a sequence response. Engineers call the method "pancaking,"

Buildings of 20 stories or more do now not topple over like timber or chimneys

Explosive fees are seen taking pictures from severa flooring really previous to crumble and one have to see flashes because the demo costs fireside off.

What human beings noticed had been now not explosions. As the floors collapsed on top of every awesome you could see home home windows, air and concrete dust being expelled out of the constructing. The panes of glass in short reflecting and flashing the slight of the sun.

Of direction there were explosions. Large houses inclusive of those contained many things which includes gasoline tanks, computers and lots of others. With fires raging indoors the ones had been at risk of explode.

Comment.

It takes months of education for expert detonation crews to set up a massive constructing for destruction - weakening structural columns, placing prices and laying miles of detonation wires in every tale of the homes. All this saved hidden from the loads of people who labored there, the place of work group of workers, protection guards cleaners. Anyone of these blowing the whistle to store themselves and co-employees from loss of life.

Why could likely the conspirators problem with bombs in addition to jetliners? (Alternatively: why trouble with jetliners further to bombs?)

Heat producing explosives collectively with thermite had been positioned within the dust.

It could have desired 100 metric thousands of thermite in plenty of small packages. The corresponding quantity of reacted thermite has in reality failed to show up.

No melted metallic or lessen beams at Ground Zero stated through humans or any proof of explosions.

From 1, hundred,000 tonnes of building materials maximum minerals are found in a few amount inside the dust. Even so, evidential evidence of thermite grow to be not placed.

What approximately the claim that metallic melts at a higher temperature than the burning temperature of jet gasoline, consequently the metal could not have melted.

Steel does no longer have to soften earlier than it fails, as it will lose about 50% of its power at 60% in their melting temperature. Plus metal attempts to amplify at both ends, but while it could no longer make bigger, it sags and the encircling concrete cracks.

No place of business fire ever made a constructing collapse.

No place of job fire have become ever as huge as those . The planes, which crashed into the houses, took out many flooring upon effect and stripped the fireproofing from the middle load-bearing structures on the ones flooring.

With approximately 28,000 Litres left in their tanks jet gasoline flowed down the elevator shafts from the top of the building, inflicting explosions and fires everywhere, whilst causing extreme damage to load bearing pillars.

The exterior steel shell and the fringe columns of the building have been penetrated so devastatingly via the planes, the form's capacity to hold itself up become threatened. So even as one ground went, the blended weight supposed all of them went.

With the center metallic columns weakened, load-bearing come to be transferred to the constructing's shell. Multiple floors weakened, sagged and eventually inflicting established disintegrate.

Evidence from the Ground Zero debris, including the big metallic columns had been speedy shipped distant places to prevent inspection.

It is sincerely documented what happened to the steel and so on. It modified into first treated through Protec and later on the Fresh Kills web website via Yannuzzi Demolition. It became months earlier than it modified into shipped to China which end up the ordinary time frame.

Israel

9-11 become surely pulled off via the use of Mossad to galvanise US help for Israel and damage their enemies and 4,000 Israelis Jews have been warned to live domestic on September 11th.

How might also want to Mossad contact 4,000 Jews and with out truely each person else understanding?

Not a unmarried Jewish character died within the attacks.

About 10% of the sufferers of the attacks have been Jewish,

It is anticipated that amongst 4 hundred and 500 Jews died inside the assaults on

the World Trade Center on 9/11. The particular range isn't recognised, considering the truth that

expert record-maintaining does now not listing the religions of the victims.

Bush became moreover already one of the most effective supporters Israel has ever had.

In reality 9/11 occurred to fall on the surrender of the month of Elul, in some unspecified time in the future of the instances most important as a great deal as Rosh Hashanah, at the same time as observant Jews might have extra prayers at their morning prayer offerings and consequently many Orthodox Jews went to paintings an hour later.

There have been, however, numerous Orthodox minyanim (prayer groups) organised within the WTC.

Actually they might certainly have waited some days till Rosh Hashanah or Yom Kippur, whilst almost no Jews could had been at paintings.

Larry Silverstein

This idea posits that WTC lease holder Larry Silverstein had virtually taken out a big insurance insurance covering his homes for billions of dollars worth of insurance in case of terrorist assaults and that Silverstein had them destroyed so he'd earnings off it.

Silverstein had presently taken out an anti-terrorism coverage at the World Trade Centre which had already been bombed as quickly as earlier than in 1993. The insurance rate modified into way under what it want to have been and the payout Silverstein acquired, of $4.Seventy seven billion, changed into an entire lot a good deal less than the actual fee of cleansing up the internet site and constructing the Freedom Tower, which totalled over $nine billion. It took federal and state loans, on the aspect of personal investment, to cover the relaxation.If it was an insurance rip-off, it turned into the worst ever.

The Pentagon Attack

A missile have become fired on the Pentagon, The outside of the Pentagon might no longer even seem like it was hit via manner of a plane. The outline of the wings wasn't there.

A crashing jet could now not punch a cartoony plane shape of itself right right into a bolstered concrete constructing. Besides, one of the plane's wings took out severa moderate posts on a nearby roadway most important as a great deal as the impact net website and sheared off even as the plane flew floor stage, the alternative certainly disintegrated on impact. Such an aircraft is on the complete empty place and will nearly have melted into the reinforced concrete with its load-bearing columns.

Two holes had been seen in the Pentagon right away after the attack. Conspiracy theorists declare every holes are a ways too small to had been made with the aid of way of manner of a Boeing 757

Pictures of the crash net web page online simply show wherein Flight 77's touchdown equipment punched a 12-ft hollow placed close to the precept hollow caused by the impact. In reality, the aircraft clearly penetrated some distance into the form.

The Pentagon has vast missile defence structures that didn't pass into movement on September 11, 2001. Why?

The Pentagon does not have a missile defence gadget. One reason is due to Reagan International Airport, it honestly is straight away inside the flight route of the Pentagon. A missile defence device might constantly want to decide if a aircraft from the airport heading in the path of the Pentagon turned into a missile. Thus there might be a severe risk of an twist of fate.

Conspiracy theorists insist there was no aircraft wreckage at the Pentagon.

There is photographic evidence and eyewitness payments of plane wreckage and harm constant with a plane crash. The the front garden of the Pentagon have grow to be scattered with huge quantities of aircraft wreckage, all of it matching up perfectly to a 757 jet plane.

Hundreds participated within the cleanup and observed every plane debris and our bodies of the passengers.

Anyone planting plane debris at the net web web page afterwards ought to had been visible.

Hundreds of humans noticed the plane circle then fly into the Pentagon.

What happened to the passengers who have been visible boarding American Airlines flight 77 and later died inside the crash? Were the passengers all taken some other place and murdered or had been they all in on it and now all the time in hiding.

Two greater crucial factors are why use a missile inside the first region? Using a plane would be easier -saves all the duvet up. Finally, any missile might have destroyed the whole constructing.

Five layers of the Pentagon were broken, now not certainly the outer wall. Some of which clearly collapsed on pinnacle of the plane.

There are photos of aircraft wreckage within the building and scattered everywhere in the Pentagon garden.

Numerous witnesses saw the plane approach. Nobody noticed a missile.

WTC7. The Third Tower

WTC7 modified into intentionally "pulled down" with explosives.

The time period "pull it" modified into used by the owner, Larry Silverstein, in a TV interview. Conspiracy theorists claim that "pull" is widespread jargon within the demolition employer to fireside off demolition expenses inside the constructing

However the terms "pull it" have become intended regarding the firefighting institution seeking to positioned the blaze out. Demolition specialists stated that the time period for demolishing a constructing is not "pull," but "shoot it" or "blow it.". They have by no means heard "pull it" used to consult an explosive demolition.

He changed into talking about pulling firefighters lower lower back. Moreover, constructing owners do no longer have the general authority over emergency private at a catastrophe scene.

So why did it collapse?

WTC 7 changed into hit through a big amount of debris, inclusive of the fringe columns of one of the Twin Towers, which tore a big 20 storey gash in the thing of the form. That damage have turn out to be obscured with the useful resource of manner of smoke in most photographic proof. By the time the evacuation order grow to be given, the slumping east facet of the structure have become knocking down the west aspect in a diagonal crumble and changed into visibly sagging.

The tower itself have come to be constructed over a power substation, so there were a high-quality deal a lot less structural columns on the decrease flooring. Losing one may have introduced approximately extreme issues.

Damaged with the resource of falling particles, the building then endured a fire that raged for hours. It could not be put out because of screw ups within the sprinkler device and there has been no water right now to be had for combating the fires. Investigators accept as genuine with the hearth end up fed for as a brilliant deal as seven hours by way of way of Diesel gas tanks for turbines, that have been inside the building. Most tanks were pretty small, however the 5th floor become related to a huge tank in the basement. The constructing had big fires burning on as a minimum six floors and different fires on at least 16 flooring. Any this form of six fires could likely were taken into consideration a massive incident within the route of everyday FDNY operations.

Three hours after WTC 7 changed into abandoned the constructing failed and collapsed.

WTC 7 become destroyed as a way to smash SEC studies documents that have been saved there.

Most files have off-web page backups of essential documents except and no important investigations that had been dropped due to destroyed files.

Flight ninety 3

The Flight 93, aircraft that became hijacked and crashed right into a Pennsylvania problem via the usage of the passengers, modified into sincerely shot down through the use of the USA Air Force with a warmth-searching for missile from an F-16 or a mysterious white plane.

This ought to either were because of the reality the Air Force knew it changed into headed in the direction of a civilian goal or to cowl the proof that the passengers were drugged or that the hijackers did now not even exist.

National Guard pilot, Rick Gibney, modified into accused as having fired missiles that introduced the plane down. Gibney, has denied any involvement in a plot.

Records show that he modified into flying over Montana on the time then flew Ed Jacoby Jr., the director of the New York State Emergency Management Office from Montana to Albany, N.Y.

At least six eyewitnesses say they saw a small white jet flying low over the crash place almost without delay after Flight 90 three went down

This modified into in fact a commercial business enterprise jet inside the vicinity and the FAA requested them to fly low to have a have a look at the wreckage and they did. They were given down within 1500 feet. Of the ground once they turned around. They determined a hole inside the ground with smoke popping out of it. They marked the place with the aircraft's navigational device, and headed to the airport.

No forensic proof has ever been placed suggesting a missile being fired.

The pattern of wreckage on the ground facilitates a aircraft crash, now not an explosion.

The mobile phone calls made via thirteen passengers on Flight ninety three during the hijacking have been faux because of the reality mobile cellphone towers can not commonly select up calls above 10,000 feet.

Evidence showed all the calls but have been made from the in-seat Airfones -which had a booster on board the aircraft.

The cell phone calls had been made at the same time as the plane turn out to be plenty lower and close to crashing.

The "fake telephone call" idea furthermore is predicated on so known as "voice morphing" or mimicking era, In 2001, it had notable worked with very small samples of speech, no longer the lengthy calls passengers had with their loved ones.

Again how many conspirators may be required in hiding or murdering the passengers, make recordings that mimic the cellular smartphone conversations of passengers, placing plane components at the "crash" websites and so forth.

Cockpit recordings suggest the passengers on United Airlines Flight ninety three teamed as plenty as attack their hijackers, forcing down the aircraft.

Flight ninety three flew into the ground, at a steep attitude, at approximately 580 mph, disintegrating maximum of the wreckage.

United Airlines flight ninety 3 became shot down through a missile and disintegrated in mid air, scattering the wreckage over a large place, indicating the aircraft have end up breaking apart earlier than effect.

Small bits of slight debris had blown simply over a mile and a 1/2 of and landed in Indian Lake. Indian Lake is not 6 miles some distance from the crash internet site online. The lake is 1.Five miles away due to the fact the crow flies; 6 miles using.

The engine fan, ended up miles from the number one crash internet page

The fan sincerely landed great three hundred yards from the internet website online online.

Chapter 5: 7/7 London Terrorist Attack

On 7 July 2005 three explosions came about on the London Underground tool: the number one on the Circle line among Aldgate and Liverpool Street, the following at Edgware Road station and the 1/3 at the Piccadilly line amongst Russell Square and King's Cross. A fourth explosion passed off at the pinnacle deck of a London bus in Tavistock Place. The suicide bombers, who were moreover killed, had been placed to be: Mohammed Siddeque Khan, Hasib Hussein, Shazad Tanweer and Jermaine Lindsay.

Various conspiracies recommend that the assaults were no longer the paintings of Muslim terrorists in any respect, but had been done thru:

The Government to decorate guide for the Iraq struggle.

Workers on the London Underground.

Richard Jones and 12 bus passengers.

Verint.

Kingstar Demolition.

Workers for the CCTV machine.

Scotland Yard.

Benjamin Netanyahu.

Mossad.

Police Commissioner Ian Blair.

People strolling in Netanyahu's lodge.

Israeli businessmen at a conference.

Photographic proof

The Fabricated photograph of them entering the Luton station.

The pole in the back of one of the bombers seems in a image to be in the front of him indicating the photo is faux..

This turned into due to freezing low great video. Video pictures is to be had of them in London that day besides.

07:40 teach from Luton to London did not run that day so they couldn't have made it to London in time.

No so that they in all likelihood stuck the earlier teach at 07:25. Besides reconstructions set up that they'll have had been given to London with sufficient time to perform the suicide attacks.

Anyway there can be video snap shots of them in London that day. (as soon as this argument is set up, then of direction they must have been patsies).

The CCTV cameras have been near down or the pix disappeared because they had been owned with the useful resource of the use of the Israelis.

Verint Systems, an Israeli organization don't really function the software program themselves, they clearly supply the goods, which incorporates to the London Underground.

And in any case considering then pix has simply been launched!

The Driving Licence

How may want to the Bus bomber's using licence be decided after he blew himself up?

The most apparent explanation is he likely left it to be located really so he might be diagnosed as a martyr. These men have been not making plans on leaving the bombs and taking vicinity the run. They preferred human beings to understand who they have been.

The Israelis Again

Benjamin Netanyahu come to be warned minutes in advance than that an attack became drawing close. Some even say that the Israel embassy end up notified in advance.

Benjamin Netanyahu, who on the time modified into the Israeli Finance Minister, turn out to be truly about to head away the Connaught Hotel in London, while a police officer outdoor stated that there had been an explosion close to Liverpool road. He modified into due to bypass the hotel adjacent to the internet site of the number one explosion, Liverpool Street train station, in which he turned into to deal with an economic summit.

If the Israelis knew this conspiracy became going to seem they might have favored to be as some distance a ways from the bombs as possible. Yet The Israeli conference went on as regular from 9am. It modified into an hour after the bomb exploded that the conference motel modified into evacuated however their essential visitors.

Associated press who at the start stated it, later said that their facts were unconfirmed and became incorrect. Mistakes rise up inside the press all the time straight away after terrorist attacks.

Richard Jones an 'explosives expert' were given off the bus just in advance than it blew up.

During the 1960s, Richard Jones worked as an electrician in an explosives production unit. He was not a chemist. He were given off the bus because it was diverted due to the chaos in London.

eleven one among a kind human beings were given off the bus quick in advance than it exploded. Or are we now considering the 12 have been a collection to cowl up what Richard Jones became doing!

The bombs were planted below the trains.

Some eyewitnesses did surely say that "tiles, the covers at the floor of the educate, all at once flew up, raised up."

There have emerge as no time to test their statements, as moments later the police widened the cordon. In the file to the Guardian it said "become believed" there were an explosion "below the carriage of the educate". It later became clear from interviewing specific passengers who've been inside the course of the seat of the explosion that the bomb had actually detonated inside the educate, not under it.

Peter Power modified into conducting a fictional "state of affairs" exercise of more than one bomb assaults on London's underground which came about at precisely the identical time because the bomb assault on July 7, 2005. This is too much of a twist of future.

It has been claimed, for example, that Peter Power's exercising worried one thousand people.

What Power definitely stated is that he turn out to be walking the exercising 'for a organisation of one thousand people'. The actual exercise worried 6 humans from a publishing business enterprise, become place of work based absolutely and simply a walk - through based on a scenario. It involved watching movies of a fictional occasion and discussing what they might do approximately it. A glorified powerpoint presentation.

Besides if it's miles claimed that the authorities grow to be at the back of the assaults, or knew they might show up, what might be received thru method of having a drill at the same time?

They did now not buy single tickets.

If you're going to London people have a propensity to shop for a tour card, which lets in you to excursion to any excursion spot and use buses and the tube.

The Canary Warf 'shootings'.

This is ready the rumour that the terrorist suspects were shot in Canary Wharf. It has been claimed that at least people found the men being shot.

Who were the ones witnesses and the way has their tale been corroborated? No one seems to recognise. Around a hundred and five,000 human beings artwork in Canary Warf. It's a pretty busy vicinity. There is not a unmarried witness to the presence of police snipers at Canary Wharf or to shootings, no longer to mention the shootings of the alleged bombers.

In Tony Blair's speech he said that 'we recognize this changed into completed in the call of Islam' in advance than all people knew for fantastic.

The police had been sad approximately him using those phrases even as the cause for the bombs had no longer been set up but. Having said that Tony Blair modified into now not the primary person to have made this bet about a terrorist assault earlier than it turn out to be showed, and he would possibly now not be the ultimate.

The Number 30 Bus

Why have become there a 'Controlled Demolition van subsequent to the bus?

Well they had been on their manner to a technique in Kent.

This enterprise enterprise doesn't even use explosives however demolishes concrete the usage of diamond tipped bits. They have no licence or knowledge in explosives.

On the aspect of the bus that end up bombed turn out to be a poster with 'Outright Terror, bold and Brilliant' on it.

This have become part of a poster for the film 'Descent' one in every of 890 buses with the equal poster.

Further remark.

Why might probably 4 friends journey from leeds through the usage of automobile collectively, get on a educate and excursion to London together and then all depart every exclusive. Funny way to spend a day ride!

Sidique Khan and Shezad Tanweer had been the trustees of the Iqra charity e-book place and children outreach organisation that looks to had been a hub for the distribution of 'extremist' Islamic media.

Sidique Khan seemingly went to a terrorist training camp in Malakand, Pakistan in 2003, and to at least one 'education camp' inside the Lake District in 2001.

Khan and Tanweer were every surveilled time and again in touch with convicted terror suspects.

Chapter 6: Jfk

On November 22, 1963, President Kennedy, Texas Governor. John Connally and their better halves have been the usage of in a gradual, open motorcade through Dallas. At 12:30 p.M, as the automobile grew to come to be onto Dealey Plaza, three gunshots rang out. Kennedy and Connally were both shot. The automobile sped to a nearby medical institution, in which the president changed into said useless and the governor modified into handled for wounds.

At about 1:14 pm, 45 minutes after President Kennedy became shot, Officer Tippit stopped Lee Harvey Oswald, who become taking walks and geared up the overall description of the assassin that turned into being broadcast via way of way of the Dallas police radio. After a short communique, Officer Tippit have been given out of his automobile and as he changed into strolling within the path of the the the front of his patrol automobile, Oswald shot him 3 times at point easy variety. Oswald changed into arrested spherical 2 PM on the Texas Theatre within the Oak Cliff suburb of Dallas. Days later, within the course of an meant switch to county centers, Oswald himself became shot and killed on stay television via a close-by nightclub proprietor named Jack Ruby.

President Lyndon Johnson appointed a fee, chaired through Supreme Court Chief Justice Earl Warren, to research the assassination. The Warren Report concluded that Oswald had fired all three pictures from a window on the sixth ground of the Texas School Book Depository, in which he worked.

The Grassy Knoll

The House of Representatives stated there was a 2nd shooter.

In 1976, the House of Representatives shaped a completely particular committee to reinvestigate the Kennedy assassination concluded that there have been a 2d shooter anyways. This turn out to be based mostly on an audiotape from a radio transmission from a Dallas policeman who'd been escorting JFK's motorcade. According to the House record, an evaluation of the tape observed out that four gunshots were fired and one of those photographs came from the grassy knoll.

However the National Academy of Sciences performed its very own evaluation of the tape and concluded that the ones four gunshot-like sounds were not gunshots the least bit.

Also the motorbike cop in query changed into not in which the House file claimed. Thus, their assessment placed the sounds somewhere other than the grassy knoll.

Nobel Prize-prevailing physicist Norman F. Ramsey stated, voices heard inside the recording indicated that the waveforms recognized as photos, had been in reality recorded approximately one minute after the assassination.

Other witnesses said that snap shots had been fired from the grassy knoll.

It is quite tough to tell the deliver of a shot thru sound of discharge of a firearm. Eyewitness perceptions of images numerous from inside the back of the limousine, (the location of the Book Depository), from inside the front or from the right facet (the grassy knoll), from right inside the President's automobile. Which isn't always sudden thinking about the Dealey Plaza has multi-storey homes on the north, south and east factors making it a virtual echo chamber. However, relatively few witnesses said that they got here from a couple of path.

People began out out dashing to the knoll indicating that the gunman have grow to be there.

However, the "rush" to the knoll really befell over a minute after the photographs. It turn out to be precipitated via using Officer Haygood, a Dallas motorbike policeman within the parade. He become a block away while he heard the primary of 3 photographs. After racing to Elm Street, he ran as heaps as take a look at with a policemen he noticed at the rail bridge. Only then did people start strolling up after him, falsely questioning he emerge as after a perpetrator.

Classic Gunman Shape

In 1967 came the declaration that a "conventional gunman" shape emerge as apparent on a frame of the terrible-quality 8mm movie taken by using Orville Nix.

Within months, Josiah Thompson had laid that one to relaxation, noting the equal shadow pattern effect in a frame taken of the equal spot prolonged after the assassination.

The Three Tramps

Who have been the 3 tramps?

There had been the "three tramps" whose snap shots have been snapped by way of newsmen rapid after cops pulled them from a railroad boxcar in the returned of the grassy knoll, who really 'disappeared'.

Well the 3 tramps had been John Forrester Gedney, Gus W. Abrams, and Harold Doyle; they had been, ultimately, tramps no matter the whole lot.

Umbrella Man

What approximately the Umbrella Man?

A mysterious determine glimpsed in numerous snap shots, popularity at the aspect of the road with an open umbrella over his head on a wonderfully sunny day.

After years of anonymity the Umbrella Man became out to be Louie Steven Witt. In his Select Committee testimony, Louie Steven

Witt recalled how had come to Dealey Plaza to heckle the President with a symbolic protest the use of an umbrella. Witt counseled the Committee that he preferred to taunt Kennedy, for Joseph Kennedy's (JFKs father) sympathy for Neville Chamberlain's famous "peace in our time" appeasement of Germany, which have come to be observe below an umbrella. Lyndon Johnson had previously chided his opponent's father, saying "I turned into never any Chamberlain umbrella man." Witt had moreover lingered in the Plaza prolonged after the assassination.

The Head Jolt

Why did the president jerk backwards on the equal time as hit in the returned of the top thru a bullet? It appeared like that lethal bullet became fired no longer from at the back of Kennedy however from in the front of him.

In the well-known images captured thru bystander Abraham Zapruder the President is shot within the head and it snaps strongly to his left. Suggesting that one of the pix got here from someplace aside from the e-book depository. Hence there had been in fact gunmen?

Neurologists had stated that a nerve completing can explode at the same time as hit via using a bullet. In this event it method there's no essential relation among in which a bullet comes from and which manner the nerve fragments fly and therefore make the frame float.

So the "head snap" modified into now not due to the actual effect of a bullet. In 1975, CBS News, which had employed a tech employer to conduct a immoderate-resolution analysis of the Zapruder film, decided that, on Frame 312, Kennedy's head slammed in advance 2.Three inches, and hundreds more rapid than it jolted backward an right away later on Frame 313.

Thus, the bullet hit his head from at the back of, nerves explode and there is a large reaction yet again and left followed with the aid of the usage of the usage of a marvel of neurologic impulses sent from the mind down the spine causing neuromuscular spasms to each muscle in the body.

Also claims that his right head wound is the get entry to wound, don't provide an reason behind the dearth of exit wound at the possibility aspect of his head.

As further proof of the bullet's trajectory, bits of the Carcano bullet were decided proper a few of the the the the front seat of the limo and the proper hand front door. It modified into badly deformed as it's been through a cranium and had marks matching it to the Carcano rifle in the Texas School Book Depository building.

Parkland Hospital frame of people

The Parkland Hospital Professionals in Trauma Room One of Parkland Hospital in

Dallas made observations indicative of snap shots from the President's the front in region of the rear.

For instance, some described a massive blowout to the rear of the top, in region of the proper the the front or that the wound in the President's throat grow to be an entrance wound, now not the go out wound.

Regular mistakes are common. A examine published in 1993 within the Journal of the American Medical Association examined 46 times related to deadly gunshot wounds over a 5 year duration. In 52 percentage of the times, errors were made in distinguishing among entrance and exit wounds and the quantity of bullets concerned.

President Kennedy's body changed into taken to Bethesda Naval Hospital in Washington in which a postmortem examination changed into executed. The studying pathologists have been hospitalists and no longer knowledgeable in forensic strategies.

The Bullets

There in reality wasn't sufficient time for Oswald to fireplace one bullet at Kennedy, then each different at Connally.

The bullet which inflicted the number one wound to the President at the lowest of the neck exited his throat and went directly to inflict numerous wounds to Governor John B. Connally, seated in the the the front of the President.

Critics generally propose that the state of affairs come to be fabricated out of skinny air so you can provide an purpose of ways a lone gunman could have fired the pictures inside the needful time, as installation via way of the Zapruder film.

Critics of this principle drew diagrams tracing the path of a bullet that might have needed to curve round in midair numerous times, in a couple of commands a terrific manner to rip thru Kennedy's neck, then into Connally's ribs and wrist so there need to had been each exclusive shooter on the grassy knoll.

FBI exams found out that Oswald's rifle is probably fired no faster than as soon as each 2.25 seconds. Either there have been at the least two gunmen—or because of the fact the Warren Report claims, Kennedy and Connally were hit by way of manner of the same bullet. This is the "unmarried-bullet principle".

The those who draw those diagrams located Connally at an same top to and seated right now within the front of Kennedy. This is incorrect, due to the truth the all over again seat, wherein JFK rode, modified into three inches better than the the the the front seat, in which Connally rode, so that you can save you Connally from blocking off the view of the president. Also they have been now not sitting inflexible and dealing with in advance however were twisted in their seats and waving on the group. Rearrange their our bodies that way and with meticulous reconstructions, the use of fairly correct 3-D laptop models, the road from Oswald's rifle to Kennedy's better returned to Connally's ribcage and wrist appeared certainly directly. There turned into no need for a magic bullet handiest the statistics of the single bullet.

Oswald without a doubt wasn't a tremendous sufficient shooter to carry out the venture.

Oswald licensed inside the Marines as a sharpshooter and after that always re-certified at least as a marksman.

Also, Oswald become firing at a sluggish-moving intention masses an awful lot less than 88 yards far from Kennedy's motorcade. Not even half of of the 2 hundred yards Marines hearth at in some unspecified time in the future of rifle qualification.

The Carcano rifle he come to be the usage of wasn't an vintage piece of junk as some have claimed however a properly-built and correct weapon which have become although in use thru Italy's rifle drill company.

Oswald's very non-public spouse claimed that he practiced dry firing the weapon all the time.

A Parkland hospital employee determined an intact bullet among the pad and steel side flange on one of the stretchers. This bullet is regularly called the "magic bullet" or the "pristine bullet." How should this be?

With the shell's close to-pristine appearance, many perplexed if it had in truth done what the Commission had said it had completed. The bullet became not determined in or round each sufferer. It changed into determined as a substitute on a stretcher at the clinic in which the sufferers had been handled. Evidence placed in advance than the Warren Commission couldn't in reality set up if the bullet changed into found on Kennedy's stretcher or Connally's.

However, the bullet become neither magic nor pristine. In truth, those phrases are misleading as it changed into appreciably distorted.

After passing through JFK and Governor Connally, it reduce the Governor's pants and driven a piece into his left thigh. Intact the bullet had fallen out of the Connally's garments and onto a stretcher at Parkland Hospital. Studies finished with the useful resource of the FBI firearms examiner forensically matched it to a rifle owned with the aid of Lee Harvey Oswald. Full Metal Jacket bullets in conjunction with this were designed to live intact and bypass through a body—correctly taking the soldier out of fight without the breaking up and causing untold butchery.

The Vietnam Connection

President Kennedy have become killed because of the reality he posed a serious risk to the warfare tool and its attendant earnings.

A National Security Action Memorandum report stated that JFK meant to withdraw from Vietnam with the aid of the forestall of 1965, beginning with the removal of one,000 advisors via manner of the give up of 1963.

Yet McGeorge Bundy, who served as United States National Security Advisor to President Kennedy said that the '1,000-man withdrawal' emerge as only a token that would in no manner were repeated. He believed it signified no shift of coverage.

The record moreover goes on to say that this emerge as great if the U.S. Military undertaking of stabilising South Vietnam's safety and finishing the repressive regulations of its more and more tyrannical government can be finished with the resource of the end of 1965. Otherwise america involvement might probably hold on.

In July of 1963, Kennedy stated, "In my opinion, for us to withdraw from that attempt ought to imply a collapse now not handiest of South Vietnam, however Southeast Asia, so we're going to stay there."

On the day of his dying he become making plans to deliver a speech on the Dallas Trade Mart reaffirming his willpower to Vietnam, and a few other 8 international locations positioned on or near the border of the Communist bloc.

The CIA

President Kennedy had threatened to "splinter the CIA into a thousand quantities and scatter it to winds" after the Bay of Pigs debacle.

Only weeks before his lack of lifestyles, JFK stated, regarding allegations of CIA misconduct in Vietnam: "I anticipate that even as the CIA can also moreover have made mistakes, as all and sundry do, on specific sports, it has had many successes which may match unheralded, for my part in this example it is unfair to rate them as they have been charged. I think they have got accomplished a fantastic job."

President Johnson appointed to the Warren Commission former CIA director Allen Dulles, who had resigned inside the wake of the Bay of Pigs.

This changed into in reality at the request of Attorney General Robert Kennedy. JFK and Dulles considerably massive each different, for JFK spoke with tremendous praise for Dulles properly after the Bay of Pigs invasion.

Oswald The Spy

Oswald's specially unusual defection to the Soviet Union in 1959 raised hypothesis via the use of writer Harold Weisberg that Oswald changed into an intelligence agent. But after almost 40 years of pioneering studies, Weisberg admittedly stated he had not located a shred of proof to guide this speculation.

Jack Ruby and the mafia connection

The reminiscences of people who truly knew Jack Ruby say he modified into no longer involved in organised crime.

Dallas Morning News columnist Tony Zoppi, who knew Ruby, said Ruby "...became a actual talker, a fellow who would possibly communicate your ear off if he had the risk. You have to be crazy to expect each person can also want to have relied on Ruby to be a part of the mob. He couldn't maintain a thriller for 5 minutes".

Ruby come to be a small-time nightclub operator, bar-room brawler, police groupie, should-be FBI informant (but the Bureau concluded that he had no useful information). There is not any evidence that Ruby had any massive dating to organised crime.

He advocated Assistant DA Bill Alexander, "Well, you guys couldn't do it. Someone needed to do it. That son of a bitch killed my President".

Jack Ruby additionally stated "some human beings are accusing me falsely of being part of the plot . . . A plot to silence Oswald. . . No conspiracy may additionally need to income with the resource of silencing Oswald in a public fashion: What's the element of putting off one suspect at the identical time as concurrently handing the police some other?".

Chapter 7: Chemtrails

In an international survey of 3015 humans, 2.6% of the respondents said they believed that there may be a mystery authorities programme that makes use of airplanes to area dangerous chemical substances into the air. 14% stated they in element believed it. The software is called 'Chemtrails'.

Those who enroll in the Chemtrail idea receive as right with that the white exhaust you note from a plane is in truth a part of a thriller authorities take a look at to spray us with chemical substances. These exhausts are genuinely high doses of climate or mind-changing chemical compounds presupposed to preserve us beneath control or poison the surroundings or lower the population counting on what you study or who you talk to.

Persistance

Why do jet contrails sooner or later persist, however your breath condensation fast evaporates?

Clouds coming from planes are the crafted from condensation of water vapour. When you breath out on a chilly day, you see a piece cloud of condensation form from your breath. But the condensation out of your breath speedy evaporates. Condensation trails from a jet can final for plenty mins, even for hours once in a while.

The distinction is because of the fact a contrail freezes.

Contrails form at -forty stages Fahrenheit (which is also -40 Celsius), or less warm. At that temperature the tiny drops of condensed water will right away freeze. Once frozen they can not evaporate and they may be too cold to melt. They can but fade away via a way referred to as "sublimation" - in which a strong will become a gas.

The proponents claim that when 1995 contrails had a one in every of a type chemical composition and lasted plenty longer on the sky.

It is properly set up by way of manner of way of atmospheric scientists that contrails can remaining everywhere from lots less than a 2nd, as a lot as numerous hours. With sufficient air traffic, it's far viable for contrails to create a wholly overcast sky and persists for hours.

The motive that one aircraft makes contrails, or makes contrails that persist, and the opportunity plane does not, is that they'll be in taken into consideration one of a kind regions of air. When the aircraft is in moist air, it makes a contrail. In dry air it does now not.

The planes depart notable trails because of the truth the planes are at distinct altitudes.

There is also masses of evidence of extended-lasting contrails proven in World

War II technology pics or maybe pictures, books and memoirs going again to 1918.

Planes loaded with barrels

Photographs of barrels established inside the passenger location of an plane for flight test display aerosol dispersion systems.

These barrels are complete of water to simulate the load of passengers (with out the use of real human beings) or cargo to test one of a kind centre's of gravity on the equal time because the aircraft is in flight. Imagine the scenario in which every body on one issue of the aircraft slowly is going to the opportunity aspect to look some remarkable sight. This state of affairs can on occasion be a volatile for the pilot.

Chris Bovey

What about Chris Bovey's video?

In October 2014, Englishman Chris Bovey filmed a video that went viral on Facebook of a organisation passenger plane touchdown on a foggy night time time, which changed into defined as emitting chemtrails.

His flight BA244 from Buenos Aires, Argentina to London, UK became diverted to Sao Paulo rapidly after departure. As the aircraft emerge as completely loaded with gas for the lengthy flight, it have become now not capable of right away land and needed to dump gasoline to lighten its load for an emergency touchdown in Sao Paulo. Chris Bovey later confessed that he without a doubt posted the video as a humorous story, that it became only a normal gasoline promote off and that the "detained 8 hours" publish changed proper into a hoax.

Patterns in the sky

How come plane contrails on occasion shape "X" styles or "grid" patterns?

In a place with some of aircraft website online site visitors entering into many commands, there may be every viable sample of lines crossing each different. In some areas in which most of the flights are north-south, they will be predisposed to be more parallel.

There are the claims that the Germans admit to doing it.

The video snap shots that is used to guide this declare intentionally mistranslates the German word Düppel (that means "chaff") to intend "chemtrail".

Jelly

What about the mysterious jelly located in Scotland?

Hans Sluiman, an algae professional at the Royal Botanic Garden Edinburgh, is happy the gel itself is not a plant or animal. Also Alex Jones, has claimed that they're spraying this inside the ones regions.

Since the seventeenth century there have been debts of a mysterious jelly discovered in Scotland and the UK.

The jelly is 99% water.

There isn't any of these things positioned everywhere else inside the international. If Chemtrails are a part of a few type of depopulation plan, why would possibly they visit Scotland and sell off the jelly?

There aren't any payments of these items falling from the sky?

Samples of air and earth

According to Clifford E. Carnicom, he claims he is analysed ground-level air samples and they contained pretty a few lousy stuff.

76 of the overall 77 Atmospheric specialists disagree that there can be any evidence to assist this idea. The one professional who spoke back positive stated the evidence they'd stumble upon modified into 'excessive degrees of atmospheric barium in an area that usually has low ranges of the element inside the soil. A far off region with fashionable 'low' soil barium. This

professional have grow to be in reality now not ruling out the opportunity of Chemtrails.

In Michael Murphy's documentary, 'What In the World Are They Spraying?' Murphy stated he tested the aluminium content material material of rain and soil and observed extra or lots less 7% aluminium, which due to Chemtrails, is higher than it must be.

That length is properly within everyday degrees due to the truth rain has an inclination to choose out up dust on its way all the way down to Earth. In truth it shows the same attention of aluminium as tests done on rain water in 1967.

Chapter 8: The World Of Conspiracy

The belief that the truth is being withheld thru folks who wield social or political energy has been around for hundreds of years. For possibly so long as there were businesses of human beings huddled together on the earth, there had been the ones who have at a loss for words if others were via hook or via crook conspiring in opposition to them. Such beliefs can sometimes cause tragic effects as became evidenced within the contemporary-day so-called "Pizzagate" ordeal some years in the past.

In case you haven't heard this story, it worried a lethal taking pictures via a man named Edgar M. Welch, who believed a wild conspiracy principle about Hillary Clinton and severa key democrats. He claimed that they have been worried with a infant prostitution ring. On the floor, the whole thing sounds so bizarre maximum wouldn't take into account it, however this man did.

Mr. Welch notion that the trafficked children were being held toward their will at the pizza joint, and he become prepared to set them free. Wishing to take topics into his very personal palms, he marched right into a pizza parlor that changed into said to be the net website on line of the abuse and commenced taking snap shots.

Welch had have a look at all this data on line. Indeed, the net has become a effective echo chamber of factors of view, evaluations, and guidelines. And from time to time they may echo decrease lower back some subjects which are absolutely inane or maybe downright fake – as changed into the case with Pizzagate.

Knowing that this man have emerge as stimulated to kill via way of manner of on-line conspiracy theorists, it wasn't prolonged earlier than calls to create extra stringent controls for conspiracy theorists have been made to the individuals who run social media systems. This sounds vital and appropriate earlier than everything look, however at the same time as you start controlling what people are allowed to say on line – and identifying what is and what isn't a conspiracy – you open up a whole new can of worms.

In such an surroundings, unexpectedly all of us who says something that a person else doesn't like need to potentially be blacklisted and labeled a conspiracy theorist. This is a chunk disconcerting, due to the fact however the truth that conspiracy theories can be fake, a few can also moreover have a kernel of reality. If we close them down outright, we would haven't any manner of information.

Also, as is the case with pretty much the entirety, even well-intentioned censoring will in the long run be met with abuse. It's human nature to make the most conditions for our gain and in our modern, fairly polarized environment, it's truly too tempting for one faction to label special humans's factors of view as being a part of a conspiracy concept absolutely due to the fact they don't consider what's being said. In truth, they will in fact recollect it to be real.

If someone gadgets to a degree of view, in recent times the primary approach of pushing decrease again is to shout on the top of their lungs (or as a minimum the top of social media) that this exchange point of view is a conspiracy concept. This has come to be specifically distressing at some stage in times wherein a situation is unfolding and no person but is aware of all the data. It's hard for the way of truth-locating to start even as human beings label you a conspiracy theorist earlier than all the statistics has even come out.

We have seen this seize 22 state of affairs stand up time and time over again now, in our politics, governance, or even in normal existence. This results in stunted highbrow increase and deprives us of freedom of idea.

If there can be to be a real try and see a state of affairs from all facets, it's higher to permit the conspiracies circle freely than to close them down outright.

Here in this newsletter, there are no fact-checkers, perception police, or gatekeepers of what you ought to consider. The purpose of this ebook isn't to sell any of the following facts as actual or fake; it's up to you to determine for yourself. Now, with that little disclaimer out of the manner, welcome to the sector of conspiracy!

There Really Were Witches at the Salem Witch Trial

We all understand the story: Salem, Massachusetts, across the one year 1692, a colonial agreement turn out to be rocked by way of the usage of a horrible hysteria that added about numerous humans being wrongfully accused of witchcraft. These terrible souls not best had their reputations maligned, however many furthermore lost their lives. But what if there's extra to this story? What if it wasn't all best a bunch of mass hysteria?

Yes, there may be certainly a conspiracy concept about the Salem witch trials that contends that there sincerely have been witches and paranormal forces afoot on the time, and that the witch hunt that transpired might not have been virtually on imaginary grounds. It seems like a exquisite premise for a notable horror movie.

This concept takes a traditional placing like Salem and a dramatic occasion together with the Salem witch trials and turns the entirety us smug contemporary oldsters recall to be actual about it on its head. But except precise material for a destiny Hollywood screenplay, it's additionally to be had fodder for some quite rich conspiracy principle.

There stays a bargain that we don't recognize about the Salem witch trials, and plenty of what we count on we do apprehend is frequently filtered thru the lens of the term in which this retelling of Salem is being informed. The Crucible, a theatrical production written thru the usage of the playwright Arthur Miller in the 1950s (at a few level inside the Cold War and at the height of Joseph McCarthy's "witch hunts" for suspected communists), is a excessive instance of this.

The Crucible receives a few matters proper, however it gets many numerous things incorrect. Arthur Miller's portrayal has a tendency to traffic in stereotypes which have been passed right all of the way right down to us over time which advocate that nobody at Salem ever practiced witchcraft, and it turn out to be all lies trumped up with the resource of the usage of sinister authority figures who had to harm harmless humans. But it emerge as more complicated than that.

For one aspect, there without a doubt have turn out to be some "witchcraft" being practiced in Salem: fortune-telling, superstitious rituals to stave off infection, and different so-referred to as "black arts." The funny element is, the real witches have been normally left by myself! Yes, you heard that right. Because preserve in mind, at some stage within the Salem witch trials, the only people who've been hanged for being a witch were individuals who refused to confess they have been witches.

Many who've been falsely accused of witchcraft perished because of the truth they refused to confess to a few issue, they hadn't executed. If the accused had truly swallowed their pleasure and made a fake confession that they practiced witchcraft, they had been unfastened to move. And plenty of them did simply that. But tragically, some of the accused who could not compromise their necessities even at pain of loss of existence, did no longer.

One Salem resident who admitted that she have become a witch changed right into a female named Dorcas Hoar. For Dorcas, there has been no dispute; she come to be extensively identified for doing all manner of witchy subjects, but earlier than the rigors befell, this by no means brought approximately lots of a stir within the network. She test human beings's fingers, she had supplied certain "miracle treatments," and she or he or he communed with familiars and spirits.

She emerge as delivered in to be puzzled at one element, and she or he or he or he denied the expenses and have come to be sentenced to be hanged. While imprisoned, she confessed, at which factor she became given a reprieve and he or she emerge as in the end permit pass. You see, that's the problem that many humans seem to miss in terms of the Salem witch trials. Salem's leaders weren't after witches who openly practiced their craft, however as an alternative those who they believed practiced their arcane arts in thriller.

Even more bizarre, the accusers in Salem on at the least one occasion in fact procured the offerings of a recognized witch that allows you to locate someone who had escaped their clutches while accomplishing interrogations in the course of witch trials. The real witch did certainly help them discover this man or woman. The escapee, however, nonetheless refused to confess they had been a witch and have been straight away finished.

Salem of 1692 become a atypical location – at least uncommon in evaluation to modern sensibilities—and lots that went on wouldn't make lots experience to us in recent times. Today, young adults wouldn't region a notable deal inventory in a superstitious game in which they dropped a uncooked egg right proper into a cup of water to determine who their future accomplice is probably. But earlier than the internet, TV, or maybe radio, this is how human beings surpassed the time.

One of the more well-known instances of the Salem witch trial saga changed into the deliberating a female named Tituba who turn out to be regarded to encourage neighborhood children to have interaction in the ones sorts of rituals. Tituba have become at the begin from the Caribbean and it turn out to be from there that she had first found "magic video games" used to divine the destiny.

Most didn't see some thing incorrect with the ones parlor hints till a puritanical preacher came alongside and knowledgeable them that their actions were nothing short of witchcraft. Considered in that slight, being a witch appears open to interpretation. So, were there without a doubt witches on the Salem witch trials? Maybe. But now, much like then, it is predicated upon for your factor of view.

Chapter 9: Is The Truth About Life On Mars Being Kept From Us?

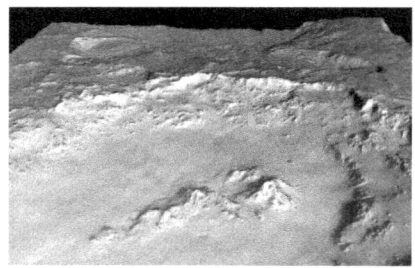

Often, a conspiracy idea stems from folks who earnestly want to trust something however are then furnished with data contrary to their was hoping-for perception. They desperately want some thing to be actual and legitimate, and then might be confronted with the fact that it is not. Most might also need to in all likelihood take transport of the data they're given and glide on. The actual believers, however, are the ones who persist.

And if the records don't align with what they accept as true with to be real, then the records are wrong – and there's a conspiracy afoot! Skeptics of conspiracy theories approximately life on Mars often use this argument to offer an explanation for the chronic belief that NASA is via the use of some technique defensive up Martian existence-bureaucracy. Among such circles, it became initially was hoping that NASA might also need to find out existence on Mars, but with every denial, the conspiracy grows that NASA is simply hiding their findings.

The Red Planet has extended been a hopeful candidate for extraterrestrial life. Scientists and laypeople alike have dreamed approximately viable Martian civilizations for hundreds of years. Some – which consist of astronomer Percival Lowell – even believed they noticed symptoms of it with their very personal eyes. You see, at the same time as Lowell seemed into his telescope one great night time in 1894, he should have sworn that he observed canals!

Canals, structures engineered to exchange the go along with the float of water, might in fact be a signal of not sincerely Martian existence, however Martian civilization. From this one intended observation, entire theories then sprang up that Mars modified right into a dry, in all likelihood death world, in which its parched populace have been forced to accumulate progressive canal systems simply to get a drink of water.

It's exciting to word, but, that inside the time that Mr. Lowell made those observations, canal-building right proper here on Earth turned into all of the rage. This changed into the era, in the end, of the Suez and Panama canals. So in all likelihood Lowell come to be projecting extra Earth-based totally absolutely completely wishful wondering than any actual Martian commentary.

Still, belief in Mars persevered via the a long time, and through the Thirties many however believed there has been functionality for Martians to be lurking someplace on our neighboring planetary body. This was dramatically set up within the 1930s on the identical time as Orson Welles made his well-known War of the Worlds broadcast.

In this broadcast, Welles have become virtually turning in a dramatic radio retelling of the H.G. Wells ebook of the identical call. It grow to be a clever version of a era fiction conventional, however probably it became a hint too clever. Taking benefit of the newness of radio, Welles had actors faux to be newshounds turning in breaking facts bulletins about a Martian invasion taking vicinity.

To be sincere, Welles did hassle a disclaimer before this device began out approximately the artwork of fiction, however many who tuned in that night time time did so after the published had already commenced out out, and for them it end up all too actual. They grew to grow to be on the radio to pay hobby what seemed like an ordinary track utility, best to concentrate what gave the impression of a legitimate breaking information bulletin.

The bulletins may want to keep over the following severa mins, every one handing over even greater ominous information approximately a regular item that had fallen from the sky, after which violent Martians that had emerged from the craft. Although in current day years the panic has been downplayed, humans had been actually extremely anxious about what they were taking note of – demonstrating both the human worry of the unknown similarly to a deep-seated willingness to virtually accept as true with that Martians are actual.

After the War of the Worlds broadcast, many entertained the opportunity that beings also can stay on Mars. The 1950s endured this concern with severa Hollywood movies exploring the idea. The United States government modified into quite curious too, for it changed into proper throughout the start of NASA that the Brookings Institute achieved an in-depth have a study as to what finding lifestyles on Mars, further to distinct planetary our our bodies, can also advise. Published in 1960, the Brookings Report referred to the consequences of a discovery of extraterrestrial lifestyles.

The document not handiest included what it'd suggest to fulfill modern civilizations, however moreover what sort of effect it would make even to find out artifacts left within the once more of with the useful resource of lengthy-dead alien species. The report entertained the possibility that "artifacts left in a few unspecified time in the future in time by way of way of those existence bureaucracy may also additionally probably be positioned via our space sports on the Moon, Mars, or Venus."

The report encouraged that such well-knownshows need to probably sell a contemporary form of brotherhood among people, inside the feel that we would revel in extra united in our commonplace humanity inside the face of a totally alien civilization. But the Brookings Report moreover issued NASA a stark warning, citing that, "Anthropological files encompass many examples of societies, high-quality in their region in the universe, which have disintegrated after they have needed to companion with formerly peculiar societies espousing terrific thoughts and one in every of a type existence methods; others that survived such an experience usually did so with the useful useful resource of paying the charge of changes in values and attitudes and conduct."

So what did the oldsters at Brookings end? They advocated that if NASA need to find out alien artifacts, they'll need to undergo in thoughts withholding that information from the general public. If that's not fodder for this conspiracy idea, I don't comprehend what's. But this modified into handiest a theoretical studies paper – there was no signal of life on Mars on the time – it turn out to be only a adventure into the hypothetical.

But for individuals who preference to believe that existence does indeed stay on Mars, it would provide what seems to be an professional possibility explanation to NASA's counseled findings. Any time NASA denies any sign of life on Mars, all they need to do is factor to the Brookings Report and shout from the rooftops, "NASA's not telling the reality due to the fact Brookings recommended them not to!"

The first robot probe sent to analyze functionality life on Mars modified into sincerely no longer sent with the useful resource of NASA, however; it become launched through the Soviet Union. Called "Mars 1," this interplanetary craft changed into launched from Russian soil on

November 1st, 1962. This probe come to be now not alleged to land on Mars however in reality fly via the planet on the identical time as taking pix of the ground and deciding on up facts on the earth's environment, radiation tiers, and — if possible — signs and signs and symptoms of organic lifestyles.

The craft made appropriate development on its way to Mars, sending back treasured statistics along the way. As the craft reached the Red Planet, it is stated to have sent back 61 extraordinary radio transmissions every few days, with critical information approximately the situations of the interplanetary space between the two worlds. But then, on March twenty first, while the craft became some sixty six,340,000 miles away from Earth, a few element took place. The radio transmission abruptly stopped.

The Soviets ought to come to accept as true with that the craft most possibly did make its flyby of Mars, but they wouldn't realise approximately it given that all contact became misplaced. The final purpose for this mishap become a smooth glitch that occurred with the craft's antenna. But conspiracy theorists have each different idea. They contend that Martians (or a few exceptional alien entity) can also moreover have close the probe down.

This, of route, brings an entire new element to the idea of a Martian conspiracy, with no longer nice human government protective up lifestyles on Mars, but moreover Martians themselves maintaining us from the fact. As absurd as this could sound, in Russia this conspiracy may additionally furthermore seem a bit extra achievable because that usa has a records of technical problems in phrases of Mars.

Several Russian craft have inexplicably malfunctioned or have even been outright destroyed even as trying to go to Mars. For some thing purpose (possibly American understanding perhaps?) NASA have end up a good deal extra a fulfillment than the Russians in its Mars missions. And it come to be NASA that could whole the primary a success flyby assignment to Mars in 1964/1965, after which launch the primary a success lander to Mars in 1976.

The phrase "a fulfillment" have to be burdened proper here, because the Soviets despatched numerous craft to Mars in the late Sixties and early Seventies, but they had been all beset with failure. The Soviets did manage to get a lander on Mars in 1971, but after a trifling 14 seconds of rolling round at the Martian ground, the lander's conversation become mysteriously out of place and in no way regained. The Soviets had invested carefully on this challenge and wonderful obtained 14 seconds of records as a stop give up end result. It seemed that some aspect gremlins had sabotaged Russia's 1962 flyby have to had been at it all over again in 1971.

NASA's Viking missions have been a good buy more a fulfillment, and in 1976, each an orbiter and a lander had been able to satisfy what they were programmed to do. While the Viking 1 orbiter waited above, the Viking 1 lander rolled round on the Martian floor snapping photograph after picture. This modified into the arena's very first glimpse of what it turn out to be like on Mars. Those wishing to discover advanced Martian towns have been in reality dissatisfied to look what seemed to be a dusty, empty purple barren area and hazy red sky – and no Martians in sight.

But some may additionally need to beg to differ, collectively with a person who used to art work at NASA. His name is Gilbert Levin, and he became once a research scientist for the gap agency. According to Mr. Levin, the Viking lander did simply come upon signs of organic lifestyles, however NASA without a doubt overlooked the findings. Levin contends that a unique take a look at to discover evidence of biology inside the soil again no longer truly one superb hit, but 4. He then defined how important this become due to the reality the records changed into being "supported through 5 numerous controls, streamed down from the twin Viking spacecraft landed a few 4000 miles apart."

Levin states that it turn out to be via the verification approach of those set controls that, "The statistics curves signaled the detection of microbial breathing on the Red Planet," Levin contends that what Viking observed taking place inside the Martian soil indicated that microbial lifestyles were gift on Mars. As to whether or not or no longer or no longer Mars has life of any shape, Levin insists that those exams want to have answered that query.

The key locating proper right here emerge as that the soil regarded to be producing carbon dioxide via a organic manner. NASA, however, rejected this idea, determining that the assessments did no longer discover signs of microbial breathing in the soil, but surely exquisite non-residing techniques that mimicked it. NASA determined that they had determined some thing that mimicked life, however changed into not life.

Chemical reactions do loads of extraordinary matters in both the lab and within the wild, so this definitely is possible. But what struck many as so weird became how brief NASA came to this surrender, and moreover, how they've got steadfastly refused to replicate the Viking experiments on destiny missions. Levin has complained about this, mentioning that whilst NASA will spend billions searching out water on Mars, they refuse to conduct extra soil locating out for microbial breathing.

As Levin placed it, "Inexplicably, over the forty 3 years considering that Viking, none of NASA's next Mars landers has carried a life-detection device to study up on those interesting effects."The query the conspiracy theorist could in all likelihood ask, of path, is why? According to Richard C. Hoagland, a self-defined NASA watchdog, that is due to the reality NASA already is privy to there's existence on Mars, however the area organisation agency doesn't want you to understand approximately it.

Hoagland has a protracted information of suggesting that NASA knows greater than it's telling. Hoagland's most well-known statement revolves around the infamous "face" on Mars. This a fixed of rock systems stretched within the direction of the floor of the planet, which, on the identical time as looked at from a nice thoughts-set, seems to take at the form of a humanoid face.

The face on Mars became first determined on July 25th, 1976, whilst a person named Toby Owen, who turn out to be walking as a undertaking scientist for NASA on the time, changed into sorting thru pics that had just been beamed once more to Earth from the

Viking venture. It changed into while he came at some stage in "Viking Orbiter 1 body 35A72," that this challenge scientist involuntarily exclaimed, "Hey, have a look at this!" As his colleagues huddled round, they, too, have been surprised at what they observed.

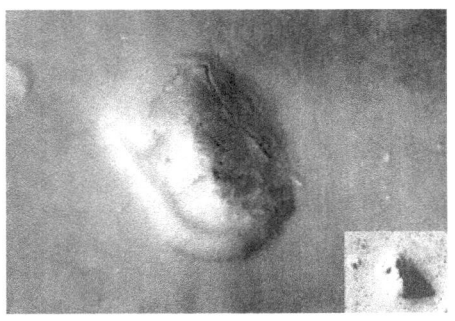

The picture seemed to capture a as an alternative ominous searching sculpture, fairly harking back to the face of the Egyptian Sphinx that guards the pyramids. If this truly changed into an alien form, it would want to be massive for it to be visible all the way up in Martian orbit. As beautiful as all this appeared to be, NASA later shrugged it off as just a trick of the digital camera, merchandise of passing shadow and light over herbal structures. Were NASA's assignment scientist's eyes simply in reality gambling suggestions on him that day? Hoagland doesn't expect so, and he spent a whole profession looking for to show that no longer excellent is the face on Mars actual, however that there are also numerous one-of-a-kind synthetic systems within the surrounding Cydonia area of Mars, which he calls the "Cydonia Complex." Hoagland used advanced imaging techniques to get close to-united statesof what seem like pyramid-type structures.

Those who trust those are herbal formations, but, contend that they will be absolutely rock formations. Hoagland is insistent that those structures are inside the form of practical alignment that they could not have come about from herbal techniques. In particular, Hoagland insists that a 500-meter shape he has dubbed the

"D & M Pyramid" is just too perfectly geometrical in shape to have truly came about from the herbal gadget of abrasion.

Even even as NASA revisited the Cydonia region in 1998 and snapped a few new pictures of the face on Mars (which regarded to expose NASA accurate in its assertions that the genuine face modified into just a trick of the moderate), Richard cried foul. The greater moderen NASA pics appearance a outstanding deal lots a whole lot much less like a face, and appear like honestly a random rock formation.

Hoagland doesn't believe this. He claims that NASA purposefully doctored the picture to do away with its distinct facial traits.

It appears that if some among us want to consider in existence – or at least beyond existence – on Mars, pretty tons not some thing will serve to influence them in any other case. Is NASA protective up Martian lifestyles and or civilization? The query will stay.

Chapter 10: Japan's Building A Robot Army

Ever for the motive that its defeat thru American forces in World War II, Japan has agreed to restriction its armed forces. Since they're allowed to have simplest a primary protection force, it is essentially as a great deal as the American army to guard Japan from functionality threats. As China keeps to upward thrust to dominance, but, the Japanese have end up increasingly worried approximately a ability war with the Chinese.

There are many reasons for this. One is genuinely proximity. Being round the corner to a developing powerhouse like China is generally going to create the capacity for the two global locations to stumble upon each unique. But the opportunity maximum vital reason is history. Many in the West aren't nicely versed inside the information of the area, however proper away earlier than and at some point of World War II, the Japanese invasion and profession of large chunks of China was one of the maximum brutal instances of violence this international has ever seen.

Japanese squaddies in large part allocated with the general guidelines of war and at the same time as encountering Chinese civilians, they raped or killed them without discretion. One such infamous attack modified into called "the rape of Nanjing," and for ideal motive, because Japanese troops went door to door all over the metropolis, brutalizing entire households. Even even though the West in huge component forgets about these objects, you'd better don't forget China has not. The residing survivors and their descendants although seethe with rage at the notion of what Japan did to them.

And now that China is in the ascendancy and Japan is in a inclined position without a normal navy, having to rely upon a every now and then-unreliable American associate, many within the Chinese communist celebration is probably extra than willing to take benefit of the state of affairs. Chinese propaganda, in fact, has grow to be increasingly anti-Japanese in current years, with some in China openly calling for belated revenge.

But Japan sincerely is in a difficult spot, militarily. Even in the occasion that they have got been allowed to craft a ordinary military pressure, the Japanese populace has lengthy been in decline with the aged outnumbering the younger people, making it tough to expect a very robust infantry – in particular one that might assignment the limitless tens of tens of hundreds of thousands of Chinese troops that they would be up toward. So, what is probably the solution to this quandary?

Japanese robots. Yes, you check that right. It has been advised that Japan may also need to certainly bridge this hollow via deploying robots on the battlefield in the destiny. While it isn't formally seemed precisely what the military heads of Japan is probably planning inside the following couple of years, Japan is already a longtime leader in terms of the usage of drones and AI in military programs.

But the usage of aerial drones and in reality having humanoid robots marching on the field are diverse subjects. Surely Japan hasn't made that jump, has it?

According to UFO researcher and lifelong conspiracy theorist Linda Moulton Howe, they've. Ms. Howe modified into giving a speech on February 10th, 2018, for a presentation she entitled, "Is AI an existential chance to human civilization?"

As she stood at the podium, she stated that at a robotics employer in Japan, four robots being advanced for navy functions shot and killed 29 scientists. She similarly contended that on the equal time due to the fact the people have been suffering to neutralize the risk, the fourth robotic linked itself to a satellite tv for pc tv for pc and commenced to construct itself stronger than it have been.

Pretty startling, proper? But as Carl Sagan used to mention, "great claims require fantastic proof." So, in which's the evidence? Well alas for this little conspiracy concept, there can be none. In conventional conspiratorial style, Howe says her supply – a meant ex-army whistleblower – for this alleged occasion has elected to remain nameless. Oh, well...loads for the robots!

Chapter 11: The Story Of The Lost Cosmonauts

According to the professional narrative of records, a Soviet guy named Yuri Gagarin become the primary man or woman sent into location, in 1961. But if you take note of a few conspiracy theorists, there is probably an entire crew of misplaced cosmonauts that went up in advance than him. These area pioneers supposedly didn't come decrease again.

It simply does create a grim picture of cosmonauts in space tablets-became-coffins, literally out of vicinity in vicinity, floating thru the cosmos for all eternity. So, why have we in no way heard of this? If the story is right, there could in reality be a top notch cause as to why it become hidden. The Soviet Union, in any case, had an extended-mounted records of overlaying up the tragic accidents of its area utility.

In 1960, for example, due to a mishap at the launchpad, seventy eight Soviets had been killed in a fiery explosion. And simply earlier than Yuri Gagarin's well-known flight in 1961, each other cosmonaut, Valentin Bondarenko, had been burned to dying in an inferno that ignited from his oxygen-crammed region pill. Unlike the West, the communist Soviets were not in all likelihood to broadcast their screw ups and mistakes. Bondarenko's fate, as an example, end up now not exposed until 1986.

Consequently, the idea that the Soviets might likely cowl up a failed first manned venture into area is at the least possible. It looks as if some detail the Soviets might likely have finished. The question then is, did they? The primary thread of this conspiracy idea surely comes from a technological know-how fiction writer, Robert Heinlein, who modified into allegedly suggested firsthand that the tale of the lost cosmonauts is real.

The idea that this account have become relayed to a author of fiction makes it seem dubious at extraordinary, but Heinlein maintained that this tale have emerge as not a work of his imagination. He said that he became travelling the Soviet Union and have become acquainted with a few Red Army cadets who showed to him that there have been a manned space release that had lengthy beyond surprisingly wrong. According to this testimony, the craft had professional a mechanical failure and its steerage device activate it within the wrong path.

I'll permit the reader determine what they don't forget this, however I need to admit this whole story sounds suspect for a huge shape of reasons. It's virtually difficult to fathom that a visitor from the West might be confided in like this. Could this have been deliberate disinformation?

At any fee, Heinlein allegedly had a few outdoor proof to corroborate the story. This got here thru the claims of unbiased radio operators in Italy who claimed to have intercepted distress calls from the cosmonauts as they drifted aimlessly in location. The radio operators who said they heard those transmissions are brothers named Achille and Giovanni Judica-Cordiglia.

According to this pair, thinking about the reality that 1957, that they had a hobby of monitoring Soviet radio signs and symptoms from place. The brothers contend that the sign they obtained that day have become an SOS transmission in Morse code. They also say that with the aid of studying the start place of the signal, they'll inform that the deliver changed into abruptly shifting similarly out into area in region of orbiting the Earth as ought to have been supposed.

But now not high-quality did they arrive up with this telemetry facts, the brothers moreover claimed to have heard the distressed voices of the cosmonauts themselves – among them, a female announcing in Russian that she ought to see flames. This became then supposedly accompanied with the aid of the disturbing sounds of the cosmonauts suffocating to loss of life. Was there a malfunction within the deliver's navigation, sending them adrift to components unknown?

There is allegedly every other cosmonaut who were given lost and whose story changed into protected up. But this one fortuitously didn't wander away in area, however as a substitute, out of area in China! Supposedly, one of the early cosmonauts – someone named Vladimir Sergeyevich Ilyushin – had a problem with navigation upon re-get right of entry to and wound up severa miles off course in a topic in the People's Republic of China. This become allegedly too embarrassing for the Soviets to ever very very own as much as, so they didn't.

So, what about the out of place cosmonaut idea? Could there be some Russian cosmonauts halfway to Alpha Centauri right now, and we don't even understand it? Most dismiss the ones type of claims as fake, and the two brothers who received the alleged radio transmissions are accused of making the whole lot up.

Some have additionally theorized that in all likelihood the brothers weren't outright lying, however had been simply confused. It has been encouraged, for instance, that possibly that that they'd sincerely picked up transmissions from early Soviet missions that launched puppies into area. Yes, the Soviets, regardless of the whole thing, did located Laika (the primary K-9) in orbit aboard Sputnik 2 in November of 1957. It has been counseled that possibly the suffocation sounds that the brothers concept they heard have become actually the dog panting. This doesn't exactly supply an motive for the sounds of the lady announcing she noticed flames, but I count on in the occasion that they had been stressed approximately Laika, they may were harassed about something else, as nicely.

The approach to this conspiratorial riddle keeps to live elusive. With such a lot of conflicting memories and with every body concerned both lifeless or extremely vintage, we can also by no means certainly realize what virtually happened.

QAnon—the World's First Fully Interactive Conspiracy Theory

Although nobody pretty is aware about the right basis of QAnon, this internet entity seems to have first emerged in October of

2017 on the message board structures of 4chan below the manage of QAnon. This is allegedly big due to the reality the patron claims to have a "Q clearance" with the U.S. Authorities, indicating that they may be "inside the recognize" as regards to categorised facts.

Several posts have been issued through QAnon alerting all who might pay interest approximately a "deep u . S . A ." searching for to intervene with the Trump manage. It moreover alleges that Trump turned into secretly recruited by the use of the navy a good way to take down this entrenched deep country equipment. According to QAnon, this is precisely what Trump's pledge to "drain the swamp" have grow to be concerning.

If all of this had been right, it would imply that there is a veritable battle occurring inside the United States government among opposing factions. As with many conspiracy theories, the QAnon precept appears to offer an reason behind – albeit in a miles-fetched manner – a number of the latest struggles taking location in society. QAnon has expertly woven collectively an tough story that paints Trump and those who comply with him as being the vanguard reputation toward the deep u . S . A ..

The QAnon conspiracy concept is complex and gives itself nearly like a hobby, giving members new clues or bits of records that Q-fans name "breadcrumbs" on a everyday basis. There is a whole secretive lingo worried with following QAnon. Q is supposedly the informant/government agent at the indoors, dropping those crumbs of information which it alternatives up from the "bakers" who maintain kneading the "dough" simply so Q has a everyday drip of facts to disseminate to the overall public.

The claims of QAnon are a protracted manner-engaging in, however possibly the strangest mindset, even for those who enjoy a top notch conspiracy concept or , is the declare that the FBI studies into Trump have become absolutely a ruse, a cowl for a larger FBI studies into Obama, Hillary Clinton, and John Podesta. This is supposed to be a coordinated example of sleight of hand on the FBI's element, virtually so the actual targets of the research – Obama, Clinton, and Podesta – wouldn't be able to rally their powerful supporters to restriction the investigators' paintings.

Yes, it sounds absolutely absurd, however that is one of the Q theories which have been promoted. As one reporter named Molly Roberts described it, "QAnon claims President Trump isn't beneath research; he is first-class pretending to be, as part of a countercoup to repair strength to the people after more than a century of governmental control by a globalist cabal."[1]

Yes, QAnon would possibly have us believe that Donald Trump is the Andy Kaufman President, pretending to be at odds together together along with his Jerry Lawler (Robert Mueller) at the same time as he's definitely busily jogging with Mueller behind the scenes inside the Obama research. For those of you who're too more youthful to undergo in mind Andy Kaufman (or haven't had the time to capture up on Netflix), he have become a comedian who specialized in setting human beings on, getting a upward push out of his warring parties, and pretending to be a few problem he wasn't.

Just analyzing those objects is enough to make one's head spin, however there are people reachable who in reality take shipping of as actual with it. And what if some of it proves no longer to be actual anyways? Well, there can be a handy little get away hatch for Q, because of the truth many have placed forth the notion that she or he effortlessly peppers some of their valid information with disinformation. Nice!

This conspiracy, therefore, can in no manner be showed or disproven. Way to go, Q!

With those theories in movement, a number of the a extraordinary deal much less solid people of society were inspired to do some pretty batty subjects. In June of 2018, for example, a person loaded up a few weapons and took an armored truck as a whole lot because the Hoover Dam, wherein he parked in the center of the road and proceeded to block website traffic. As the media scrambled to the scene, he can be visible with a sign that have a look at, "Release the OIG Report."

This come to be all reputedly in reference to a QAnon placed up that stated that there was a "labeled Office of Inspector General document" which held damning facts about the DOJ and Democrats who had attempted to restrict Trump's triumphing of the 2016 election.

These topics reputedly skip both methods, however, due to the fact only a month later some different man – moreover apparently stimulated by means of way of a QAnon located up – commenced out issuing verbal threats in competition to President Trump and a number of his family. Upon being arrested, the individual claimed he became stimulated both through QAnon and the voices which the CIA had planted in his head.

QAnon is unstable no longer handiest due to the things they may be pronouncing, however because of how addictive the parable international they have got created is. QAnon gives itself as a shape of function gambling, detective enterprise in which each person who receives at the internet and peruses thru the clues can work to solve the thriller. And what's the thriller? The thriller is whatever you want it to be in the period in-between. That's why QAnon is this type of regular beast – it's no longer clearly one conspiracy concept, it's a legion of constantly evolving conspiracy theories.

In a few strategies, QAnon can be visible due to the fact the vicinity's first in reality interactive conspiracy precept. Sure, there are high-quality set parameters about the deep kingdom and the alternative actors worried, however the rest of it's far like a large "choose out your personal journey" story of conspiracy wherein any consumer can bypass in any course for the duration of their search for the "truth." Whatever they expect that might be.

One of the more worrying theories created thru (or via) QAnon end up the so-known as Hawaii Missile Alert/False Flag conspiracy precept said to have taken place on January thirteenth, 2018. This conspiracy idea revolves round an incident that maximum humans have probable prolonged forgotten approximately, but it's a excessive one all of the equal. During the center of all the saber-rattling amongst Donald Trump and Kim

Jong Un of North Korea, on the morning of January 13th, 2018, Hawaii had a fake alarm of an coming close to near missile attack.

The media later confident us that this had only been an blunders of Hawaii's early warning machine – a faux alarm, no cause to be involved. If the media desired to allay the worries of Hawaiians it changed into a touch too past due, due to the fact the mobile mobile phone of really every unmarried person at the island had come to existence with the alarming message, "EMERGENCY ALERT! BALLISTIC MISSILE THREAT INBOUND TO HAWAII. SEEK IMMEDIATE SHELTER. THIS IS NOT A DRILL."

It took a whole terrifying 38 minutes for Hawaii's Emergency Management Agency to retract the message and announce that the alert modified into by way of twist of destiny despatched out with the aid of using manner of 1 in every in their employees. You can only don't forget how Hawaiians want to have felt. During the alert, they desperately scrambled to discover an area to cowl, knowledgeable their families they cherished them, and prepared themselves for nuclear annihilation.

All of this, only to emerge as clearly enraged on the stupidity of Hawaii's emergency offerings after they decided out it turn out to be best a large mistake. One Twitter consumer likely expressed this enraged sentiment exceptional after they published, "How do you 'thru twist of destiny' ship out an entire f**** emergency alert that asserts there's a missile coming to Hawaii and to take cover. And [then] take thirty mins to accurate?!"[2]

The worker who tousled and brought about all this chaos was later fired and maximum concept it changed into the prevent of the story. But no longer so for QAnon! The subsequent day, QAnon insinuated that the faux alarm in Hawaii changed into truly actual however the whole thing, and public officers and the media had been mendacity approximately it. What? The missile have become actual? But there has been no missile, right?

QAnon then clarified this splendid concept on February eleventh, putting forward that there has been a brand new faux flag missile attack supposed to start a battle. Yes, consistent with QAnon, the deep usa become working time beyond regulation to drag Trump right right right into a conflict with North Korea. So, if the missile changed into not a fake alarm, and North Korea didn't shoot off a missile, who did? According to this QAnon conspiracy principle, there has been a rogue CIA submarine (yes, you take a look at that right) lurking round Hawaii, making ready to release a missile.

It's said that QAnon published, "Ask yourself, if a missile have grow to be released through rogue actors, what's going to be the cause? The purpose might be to create a faux flag assault in which blame can be pinned on a reputable state actor capable of launching a ballistic missile that could hit Hawaii: North Korea. The 'rogue actors' absolutely chargeable for the assault, might thereby have created a situation wherein the U.S. Military may want to have been forced to respond."

So, if the CIA took a submarine and launched a missile, what took place? According to QAnon, the U.S. Army effectively shot the missile down over the ocean, thereby warding off disaster. According to this conspiracy precept, Trump knew all approximately it, and people spherical him have been taken aback that he did now not proper away order a retaliatory strike on the supposed beginning vicinity of the missile.

According to this conspiracy principle, the aspect of the complete ordeal have end up to make Trump expect North Korea had lobbed a missile at Hawaii and then goad him into attacking the rogue united states of america. Trump did now not take the bait, but, and refused to retaliate. It changed into supposedly then that the deep state determined to have their media puppets create the faux alarm tale – and Trump made no public comment on the situation.

This is one of the wacky QAnon theories on hand that has acquired massive flow into. QAnon frequently refers to the CIA as "Clowns in Action" or truly "Clowns" for quick. And in several posts Q has said the "clowns" taking rogue movements with a submarine to spark a battle. The funny issue about all this is that it almost reads like a 1/2-baked plot that's been stolen proper out of the script for "Red October."

Anyone with a penchant for early-1990s minutiae would possibly bear in mind that this film. It come to be released in 1990, right earlier than the autumn of the Soviet Union, and it handled a rogue Soviet submarine which defected from the Soviet authorities and commenced out to carry out nefarious moves of its private accord. Is the CIA experiencing their very personal model of a Red October, or is all this just the fabricated from some board bored 4chan poster's imagination? We can handiest bet.

Chapter 12: Saddam Hussein Had A Stargate

In 2003, the USA invaded Iraq. Even from a non-conspiratorial point of view, the motives for this invasion are a piece murky. According to George W. Bush, this changed into a preemptive strike in opposition to his so-referred to as "Axis of Evil." Bush had diagnosed Iran, Iraq, and North Korea because the maximum risky usa actors whilst it got here to U.S. Interests.

Bush's manage then went into overdrive trying to expose that Saddam had weapons of mass destruction. The evidence become lacking, however Bush hammered domestic the issue that no matter the reality that detractors have been searching out a smoking gun, they need to hurry up and get with this tool, lest it come inside the form of a mushroom cloud over New York City or some specific American target.

But however all of this fearmongering of Hussein having nuclear guns, organic weaponry, and all manner of different guns of mass destruction (WMD), after the troops went in, secured Iraq, and overthrew Saddam, there were no WMD everywhere to be seen. What came about to them? Did that wily Saddam flush them down the rest room at the closing minute? Perhaps he chucked them via a stargate.

Yes, a stargate. After Saddam was decided to haven't any WMD on hand, one of the craziest theories superior for the real purpose for the conflict was this loony bit about Saddam having a stargate – a portal to 3 one-of-a-kind international – right in his very very own backyard. Iraq, anyways, is an exciting location with pretty some statistics. In truth, it turned into the area wherein recorded human records started out.

Ancient Mesopotamia is the deliver of our oldest recognized human writings. And in case you agree with the likes of ancient astronaut guru Zecharia Sitchin, those ancient information hold a few starting records approximately site traffic from beyond. These internet site site visitors supposedly instructed historical Iraqis (Mesopotamians) approximately all way of superior generation, and one of the subjects they taught these ancient people about became stargates.

According to legend, those gates have been utilized by a tough and fast of extraterrestrial beings (the ancients referred to as them gods) called the "Anunnaki" who positioned them in location so they'll effortlessly transport themselves (and a few element else they wanted to deliver with them, along with WMD, in all likelihood) from their home global of Nibiru to ancient Iraq.

Although skeptics would assist you to comprehend that each one the bizarre myths and legends recorded in the historical writings of Mesopotamia have been virtually that – myths and legends – Sitchin and particular ancient astronaut theorists beg to differ. They do not think it end up all in reality an early shape of technology fiction; they experience that what the ancients documented modified into technological knowledge reality. For the ancient Mesopotamians, what they wrote have end up about actual-life sports, and consequently, stargates are real.

And as for Saddam's stargate? Well, in step with legend, the region's last functioning stargate may be located buried below the dust of the ancient Mesopotamian town of Nasiriyah, a few 225 miles south of

Baghdad. The form supposedly sits on pinnacle of an ancient ziggurat (a Mesopotamian-styled step pyramid). But even though the stargate modified into intact, no person reputedly knew quite the way to apply it.

Nevertheless, Saddam, not in search of to percent his stargate (the large infant), supposedly moved it to an underground cave device so that you can cowl it from the relaxation of the world. The idea goes that america got sick of Saddam hiding this gem from them in order that they launched a struggle to get the stargate for themselves. Nope, it wasn't over WMD, it wasn't even over oil – the war in Iraq became over having the privilege of hopping into a stargate to mention hiya to the mother and father on Nibiru!

More particularly, the theorists contend that the struggle modified into over fear of what Saddam might possibly do with the stargate himself. According to this conspiracy idea, Saddam have been operating very hard to restore the ruined temple complex wherein the stargate were decided, and had poured a ton of studies into the stargate to peer if he can also need to decide out a manner to get it up and going for walks yet again. This come to be supposedly Saddam's very very own mystery little Manhattan Project inside the works.

As the concept goes, spherical 2003, Saddam's institution of scientists made some kind of leap forward and have become at the verge of creating the stargate operational. This is supposedly what triggered the united states to come down on him like a ton of bricks.

Even if you have been to entertain the possibility that this wild conspiracy idea is real, commonplace feel ought to assist you to apprehend that Saddam ought to now not are becoming the stargate surely up and taking walks by the point of the invasion, because of the fact if he had a walking stargate, wouldn't he have stepped thru it? Rather than being decided cooped up in a dirty hollow inside the ground?

Another weird issue of this tale is the claim that the destruction of the Space Shuttle Columbia is come what also can associated with all this. You may moreover recall that in 2003, proper on the eve of the Iraq struggle, the Space Shuttle Columbia disintegrated upon re-get entry to into Earth's atmosphere. The bypass backward and forward grow to be destroyed and all the astronauts on board died.

Well, guess what? Those who accept as true with that Saddam had as a minimum a partially functioning stargate suggest that it modified into the dictator's ET pals who had one manner or the other shot the go back and forth down. After the tragedy, a defiant Saddam did certainly gloat a touch bit, putting ahead that God had punished the

Americans. Or did he advocate to mention that the Anunnaki had punished them?

The Founding Father Who May Have Been a

Double Agent

History knows Benjamin Franklin as a extraordinary diplomat and fact seeker – and in the long run, a founder of the us of America. He have become moreover an resourceful inventor, an avid creator, and an all-spherical particular man that every one Americans need to recognize and appreciate. Or so we had been advised.

But what most do not understand is that Franklin become additionally a hold close of subterfuge and espionage. Yes, call him the James Bond of his day – Benjamin Franklin took detail in plenty of clandestine missions on behalf of numerous handlers. Franklin served in masses of critical roles within the early United States, serving at numerous times as Postmaster General and Clerk of the Pennsylvania Assembly. But he additionally served because the colonial agent in London for Massachusetts, Pennsylvania, and Georgia.

These more than one roles created a massive network of contacts that Franklin might be capable of tap into for the duration of his career. In 1775, on the eve of revolution, Benjamin Franklin determined to throw his lot in with the revolutionaries, resulting in his intimate participation in the introduction of the "Declaration of Independence." Yet it have turn out to be moreover at some point of this time that he started operating as a secret agent, for it became Franklin who set up the so-known as "Committee of Secret Correspondence."

This committee turned into installed to benefit intel from American-first-class operatives in Britain and unique European nations. It end up through this network that Benjamin the spymaster got here inside the route of a person by means of manner of manner of the choice of Julien Alexandre Achard de Bonvouloir. Julien have become a European palms issuer who wanted to promote guns to america. The coins-strapped Americans honestly have to use a few firepower, so this modified into definitely no longer an possibility they might have handed up.

But appears are often deceiving. It seems that de Bonvouloir changed into not being absolutely honest approximately his heritage. In fact, it have become all a ruse, and de Bonvouloir grow to be a completely unique intelligence operative jogging for

France. He were tasked with infiltrating the Americans through the French Foreign Minister Charles Gravier, Comte de Vergennes. De Bonvouloir then confided with Franklin that it have become the purpose of the French to useful useful resource the Americans in the course of the British. Seeing a golden possibility, Franklin didn't hesitate to lend his ear. He moreover gave him pretty a mouthful.

He started out to embellish simply how sturdy the army strength of America modified into, and laid subjects on as thick as viable within the hopes that the French should pop out at the side of the us. He grow to be in the long run a success in the ones dreams, and the French did absolutely in the end input a proper alliance with the usa.

At the very equal time he modified into engaged with the French, Franklin modified into also frequently hopping at some stage in the English Channel to attend the infamous Hellfire Club in England. Here, he could run into British double or even triple sellers and function first-rate concourse with them as properly. In this topsy-turvy global of espionage, masses of Franklin's American friends had a hard time maintaining up. Many confused Franklin's loyalty and at times puzzled whether or not or now not he grow to be their spy, or if he became spying on them. But on the stop of the day, what without a doubt mattered modified into that Benjamin Franklin got outcomes.

Nevertheless, specific founding fathers but can also have had their reservations, even after the war have turn out to be over. Perhaps this is the reason why this founding father by no means have emerge as president. His face graces the the front of the $one hundred invoice, but he wasn't pretty trusted sufficient to take a seat down within the oval office. Franklin changed into someone of many hats, and information remains in search of to determine him out.

Chapter 13: The Advanced Aerospace Threat Identification Program

For a few detail motive, the New York Times has a long history of being on the leading area in terms of publishing bombshell cloth as it relates to the opportunity of alien existence. It turn out to be the New York Times, anyhow, that published the findings of the Brookings Report in 1960, which first counseled to the general public the possibility of such subjects, while concurrently recommending that such information be withheld from them within the name of countrywide safety.

Flash in advance to December sixteenth, 2017, at the identical time because the New York Times randomly dropped a tale called "Glowing Auras and 'Black Money': The Pentagon's Mysterious UFO Program." Right at the same time as all and sundry modified into distracted thru the Christmas vacations and the modern-day outrageous factor that President Trump said, the New York Times revealed this bizarre tale approximately how the U.S. Government has been secretly reading UFOs because of the truth 2007.

For five whole years, from 2007 to 2012, this software often siphoned off 22 million bucks from the as soon as a year rate range in order to analyze a phenomenon most dad and mom concept didn't exist. This turn out to be seemingly completed at the behest of former Nevada Senator Harry Reid, and billionaire researcher Robert Bigelow. Even after professional funding ended, it's far now been disclosed that the studies persevered — and as a ways as everybody can tell, maintains in a few shape to this very day. For what? What's reachable that has piqued the Pentagon's hobby?

The U.S. Navy has seemingly encountered some quite ordinary topics in current years that can't be and now not using a trouble defined. One of the maximum famous of these encounters occurred in 2004, and was captured on each video and radar. Known because of the truth the "Tic Tac" UFO, this craft seems to defy physics as it movements at fantastic speeds, most effective to reveal and forestall on a dime. You can also concentrate the greatly surprised reactions of the pilots as they are trying to tune the quick-shifting craft. At one trouble one shouts, "What the hell is that?"[3]

You can concentrate the priority and uncertainty in the pilot's voice. The audio thing is form of extra convincing than the video, for the reason that sound of a seasoned pilot being spooked like this is compelling in and of itself. The encounters had been leaked some years preceding to the 2017 revelation, however as is constantly the case, one in no manner is aware about what to recall on the subject of UFOs. Could they were faked? Was it a hoax of a few type?

Well, it took the Pentagon getting worried to dispel the notion that they had been fakes. Because that's precisely what came about: the Pentagon, for some factor reason, felt it changed into critical to confirm that the movement pix are real. In 2020, the Pentagon issued a statement through their respectable spokesperson Susan Gough to announce that the gadgets at the video were right, and stay unidentified – in one of a type phrases, they're bona fide UFOs.

The idea that the Pentagon could even hassle to weigh in and verify that movement images showing purported UFOs are actual is weird in and of itself.

In preceding many years, the Pentagon tended to debunk UFO stories, no longer validate them. So what offers? Why should they even problem? It seems that the Pentagon has been doing some quite heavy studies into this discipline. In January of 2019, the world discovered out what some of that studies entailed whilst on January 16th of that three hundred and sixty five days, at the behest of a Freedom of Information Act request, the Defense Intelligence Agency found 38 research packages that have been accomplished. Among splendid topics, the Pentagon modified into interested by "traversable wormholes, stargates, terrible energy, and invisibility cloaking."[4]

These revelations are so bizarre, it's difficult to consider them even upon taking note of it immediately from the horse's mouth. The most beautiful revelation via an extended manner then came within the summer time of 2020 whilst the New York Times dropped every other story indicating that the Pentagon had off-worldwide cars in its possession. It did so with the useful useful resource of way of reporting on the claims of an astrophysicist named Eric W. Davis, who said that certain debris recovered had happy him that "We couldn't make it ourselves."[5]

He then went on to signify that he had briefed officials approximately off-worldwide vehicles now not made on this Earth. The New York Times then ran a few terms from the former Senator from Nevada, Harry Reid, making it appear that he confirmed what this physicist had stated. "Off-global," of path, can most effective suggest one problem – that some thing the ones craft are, they belong to denizens from each other planet. For many, this seemed to be a totally closing affirmation that not handiest UFOs, however furthermore extraterrestrial beings, are in fact actual.

But now not so fast, parents, because of the reality only a few days later, the New York Times issued a retraction affirming that they'd misquoted the precept supply in their records: former Senator Harry Reid. Initially, Reid have become quoted as announcing that he "believed that crashes of automobiles from other worlds had took place and that retrieved materials have been studied secretly for many years."[6]

The New York Times then revised this to study, "[Harry Reid] believed that crashes of devices of unknown foundation also can additionally have took place and that retrieved substances need to be studied."[7] If you may observe wherein I placed my italics within the before and after costs, you may recognize why this moderate alteration made this form of massive difference. Initially, the NYT portrayed Senator Reid as pronouncing that crashes had happened and that the crashed UFO's have been studied.

The revision then changed Reid's sentiments to being that he concept that UFO crashes also can additionally have passed off. And inside the bizarre risk that that they had, that they have to be studied. Reid went from confirmation of an event, to simply wistfully thinking that such subjects may additionally have came about and if so, they must be seemed into. In unique phrases, the UFO saga went returned into the shadows once more, and but can neither be showed nor denied.

Interestingly, this isn't always the primary time that a newspaper has had to stroll lower back a seeming disclosure approximately the authenticity of UFOs. The infamous Roswell crash of 1947 noticed a similar retraction. A few days after some thing it grow to be crashed on a ranch in Roswell, New Mexico, a newspaper really got here out with the headline "RAAF Captures Flying Saucer on Ranch in Roswell Region."